Quilling
Paper Art for Everyone

Betty Christy
and
Doris Tracy

Henry Regnery Company · Chicago

Library of Congress Cataloging in Publication Data

Christy, Betty.
  Quilling: paper art for everyone.

  1. Paper quillwork.   I. Tracy, Doris, Joint author.
II. Title.
TT870.C52   745.54   74-8481
ISBN 0-8092-8843-5

Dedicated to Frank

Published by Henry Regnery Company, 114 West Illinois Street, Chicago,
  Illinois 60610
Manufactured in the United States of America
Library of Congress Catalog Card Number: 74-8481
International Standard Book Number: 0-8092-8843-5

Contents

Introduction

Quilling, also known as paper filigree, paper mo-
saic, or paper lace, is the art of rolling thin strips of paper into
various shapes and using the shapes to form designs. The use
of the term *quillwork* to describe this decorative art seems to
be American in origin. In her book, *Traditional American
Crafts*, Betsey Creekmore speculates that the term came into
use because in early work the paper was rolled around the
quill of a feather. Another possible origin for the term is sug-
gested by Webster's definition of quilling as "a band of material fluted into small ruffles so as to resemble a row of quills."
Fluting formed an important part of the design in many early
American paper filigree pieces.

Today's craftsman is more likely to use a pin or a toothpick
to roll the paper, and, of course, has a greater variety of
papers to use. But the craft remains essentially the same. A
strip of paper can be rolled, twisted, or bent into many
shapes. The shapes most used in quilling are coils, cones,
flutings, spirals, scrolls, and *volutes*. A *coil* is a paper strip

wound into concentric rings. A *cone* is a rounded, geometric shape that rises to a point. *Flutings* are grooves, channels, furrows, or ruffles. In a *spiral* (or *helix*), the paper is curled in a long vertical roll. *Scrolls* and *volutes* are graceful, open rolls such as those found in spiralled sea shells or on Ionic columns.

The forms and shapes that fit together to make quilled designs are stylized and fairly limited by their material—narrow strips of paper. The learning process for quilling is very simple; it consists mainly of practicing the rolling until one gets a "feel" for the proper handling of the paper strips. This "feel" is necessary to maintain the correct tension so that a coil will behave in the desired manner.

Once the quiller has mastered the rolling or coiling, he is on the way. The final result is governed by the length of the paper strip used and by the manner in which the quiller manipulates the paper. If each member of a class learning to quill puts together a flower, with each student using the same amount of the same kind of paper and following the same instructions, no two flowers in the room will look exactly alike.

Once the technique of coiling is learned, the possibilities for creativity are boundless. It is the combination of coils that defines the art, and the artist has a great deal of freedom to work with the shapes. Modern quillers have only begun to discover the possibilities open for design. They are experimenting with, reproducing, and learning from old quilling designs, and they are inventing and creating new forms. One of the happiest discoveries made by a person who learns to quill is that even though the technique is so simple that it can be acquired by anyone of any age and level of skill, it has unlimited creative potential.

In this book, we will introduce you to this fascinating craft, beginning with some beautiful historical examples of quillwork. We will deal with where to find materials, how to produce the shapes, how to create a simple project, how to display and enhance your projects, and how to create your own designs. In the last chapter, we have provided some patterns for you to adapt as you begin quilling. We predict that very soon your own creativity will blossom and you will begin producing your own designs.

Throughout the book, we have included pictures of all kinds of quilling and paper filigree. These finished pieces range from very simple, attractive designs to elaborate, elegant objects. We have included as large a variety as possible in order to offer you a broad realm of ideas to spark your imagination and enthusiasm. When you have finished this book and get into the challenges and pleasures of quilling, you are in for another surprise. A piece of quillwork in its finished state has an exciting three-dimensional effect that is impossible to describe entirely by words—even the camera does not capture its true beauty.

Finally, be careful! As many people have discovered for themselves, quilling is habit-forming. You may even become addicted!

Betty Christy
Doris Tracy

Picture of castle, English. Dated 1789. 16 by 11½ by 6 inches. The resemblance to mosaic is strong in this towered castle made in yellow, cream, gold, and blue paper. The castle is three-dimensional on a stone and shell base. A silk swag is draped across the top and down the sides; blue and red flower forms are in the upper corners. Courtesy, Colonial Williamsburg Foundation.

1 *Quilling History*

Who invented quilling? Where did it come from? How long has it been in existence? The answers to these questions are not easy to find. Since paper filigree was never a major art form, there is not much documented information available. Paper is fragile, so very few examples have survived in museums and art collections. It is surprising that even a few historical quillwork examples are extant, considering the extreme care that was necessary to keep the paper intact.

Quillwork probably originated in the elaborate filigree work that has been part of our art heritage since ancient times. Filigree work has been found on ancient Egyptian, Greek, and Etruscan tombs. Later, this open work was made of fine wires formed in lacy scrolls, arabesques, and leaves. The arabesques are fancifully interlaced patterns representing foliage, fruits, flowers, and some animals and figures. These patterns might be geometric and linear or gracefully flowing, twining, and spiraling. Arabesque ornamentation has been found on ancient vases, pillars, mosaics, ornamental lettering, and in almost any kind of decorative artwork.

*Reliquary. French. Nineteenth century.
Collection, Françoise and Guy Selz,
Paris. Photograph by Helene Adant.*

Filigree was at its finest form in Byzantine Greece during the fourth and fifth centuries and in Italy during the seventeenth century. Possibly as early as the thirteenth century, nuns and members of monastic orders began to use paper filigree to decorate reliquaries and medallions with elaborate designs. Paper coils, when rolled loosely and placed on edge as they are in quilling, resemble metal filigree, particularly when the exposed edge of the paper has been gilded or silvered. The gilded paper coils look enough like wire or metal to have fooled even art experts at first glance. When the paper is left in its natural creamy color, the coils appear even from a short distance to have been carved from ivory or very fine wood. The rolled paper strips simulate beautifully the more costly materials of Renaissance filigree work.

Mosaic is another art form that quilling resembles. Mosaic work was used by both the Greeks and Romans and reached its most elaborate forms in Persian and Turkish designs and in Byzantine art. Mosaics are formed by inlaying small pieces of marble, glass, colored stones, or other material in cement to make a picture or design. Because quilling designs are also made of small pieces fastened together in a surface design, they adapt well to mosaic patterns.

In its resemblance to filigree and mosaic, early quillwork showed the influence of Byzantine art. At the height of its power, the Byzantine Empire, with its capital at Constantinople, controlled most of the land around the Mediterranean Sea, as well as large portions of Asia Minor and Eastern Europe. The Byzantines refined the arts of mosaic and filigree to an extraordinary degree, as can be seen in the elaborate churches of the period. Later, when the new military power of Islam began to conquer the increasingly weak and decadent empire, Byzantine artisans and craftsmen fled to Europe, taking with them their valuable skills and introducing even more Byzantine elements into Western religious art. In addition, they carried with them the elaborate arabesques and floral designs of Islamic art.

The history of quillwork is, of course, also closely connected with the history of paper. Paper was invented in China in 105 A.D., and was taken to other Eastern countries during

Rolled paper work. Continental European. Late seventeenth century. 16 by 14¼ by 2½ inches. This coat of arms of paper filigree has festoons and frame of rolled paper. It is made gold with red on red velvet. Courtesy, Art Institute of Chicago.

the eighth or ninth centuries by the Moslems, who captured some Chinese papermakers on one of their forays. The knowledge of papermaking spread west, through the Moors of northern Africa and through the caravan trade or the silk route. By 1150 A.D. there were paper mills in Italy and Spain. France had at least one mill in 1189; Germany had one in 1291; and England had one in 1320.

All these developments in the history of art give credence to the hypothesis that quillwork, or paper filigree, was first used to decorate churches. Paper was not as expensive as precious metals; the paper forms were adaptable to the styles of mosaic and filigree; and the development of Renaissance art coincided with the invention and manufacture of paper. Various travelers in Europe have reported seeing elaborate paper filigree work in old churches, but no one seems to have documented any of this information. In fact, if rolled paper filigree was used in convents and monasteries as embellishment for religious articles, many of the items were smaller objects that probably are not readily accessible to the usual tourist-traveler. Or, perhaps no one has given much thought to a decoration that might have appeared to be a carving of wood or another mosaic or piece of filigree.

French reliquaries, in general, were made in convents in the region of Arles. During the nineteenth century, reliquaries were made to venerate the saints and godly people and many included fragments of bones of such persons. The pictures are beautifully made of colored papers edged in gold.

A few very precious boxes are still in existence, which were the work boxes for the nuns in the convents. The boxes contained long compartments for arranging the strips of paper according to color and size. The papers were taken out with tweezers or pinchers and then rolled and glued into position in the pictures.

Written information on quillwork is sketchy and difficult to find, especially for older European examples. The written studies of quillwork available in the United States are observational in nature—few drawings or photographic records have been made. This research primarily covers individual pieces such as framed panels, tea caddies, cabinets, coats of arms, and other such items found in museums and private collec-

Ensemble of the reliquaries of the nineteenth century. Collection, Françoise and Guy Selz, Paris.

tions in the United States and England. None of these pieces seem to be dated before the middle of the seventeenth century.

In 1929, *Antiques* magazine printed an article on "Rolled Paper Work," by G. C. Rothery. The article includes photographs of ten quillwork examples found in English museums and private collections, including five pictures of quillwork items from the Sir Gerald Ryan Collection: a piece of Spanish filigree enclosing a monastic seal; an Italian medallion framed with paper filigree; two heraldic arms, one Continental and one English; and a filigree paper picture depicting a house of the Queen Anne period.

The five remaining photographs in this article are of a paper filigree passion cross from Mrs. Layton's collection; two paper filigree tea caddies from the Victoria and Albert Museum; and a framed wax portrait and a cabinet on a stand from the Lady Lever Art Gallery.

The cabinet, pictured here, is the main piece of filigree work in the Lady Lever Collection. The front and sides are decorated in imitations of mosaics with birds, butterflies, and flowers surrounding some prints similar to those of Morland. The insides of the doors have panels of flowers painted on white satin, and these panels are decorated with flat glass beads. The doors enclose fourteen drawers and a small cupboard, each of which has a different ornamentation done with beads and rolled paper. Inside the cupboard are five more small drawers, also decorated. The legs of the stand are tapered; and both the legs and the body of the stand are ornamented with filigreed paper.

Cabinet on stand. English. Late eighteenth century. The front and both sides of this cabinet are decorated with rolled paper work resembling mosaic. The stand is ornamented in the same manner. Inside, the drawers and cupboard door have variations of design in rolled paper and beads. Courtesy, Trustees, Lady Lever Art Gallery, Port Sunlight.

13

Rothery describes the earlier examples of rolled paper work as being more irregular on the surface and using more cone shapes and other projecting parts. This sounds much like the type of work that is found on the sconces that are the most frequent examples of quillwork in the United States. He describes the late eighteenth-century and early nineteenth-century examples as being more comparable to a delicate *fretwork* (an ornamental openwork in relief).

In 1951, G. B. Hughes published an article on English "Rolled Paper Art" in the magazine *Country Life*. According to

Cribbage board. English. 1790-1810.
Oval, 7½ by 5⅜ by 1¹/₁₆ inches. The
medallion in the center is a colored
stipple engraving. Framing the picture
and filling the center of the board is
rolled paper filigree work in gold,
blue, and pink. Courtesy, Colonial
Williamsburg Foundation.

Hughes, whenever metal filigree was popular there was also a rise in the use of the paper substitute. Before the Reformation, paper filigree in England was used primarily for church decoration. In English churches during the fifteenth century, filigree scrolls of parchment and vellum formed an enriching background to religious statues. During the Restoration, in the late seventeenth and early eighteenth centuries, rolled paper was revived as a minor art, though it was no longer religious in nature. Another minor revival came in the late eighteenth and early nineteenth centuries. Fashionable Regency and Victorian ladies learned quillwork, as they learned needlepoint and other handcrafts, to fill up the long, boring hours between their more exciting social events.

Paper filigree was substituted for the more expensive paintings in wall hangings and panels during the seventeenth century and during Queen 'Anne's reign. In the Lady Lever Art Gallery is such a panel portrait of Queen Anne, with a wax face, bust, and hands. The entire elaborate costume is done in tiny scrolls and rolls, as are the backdrop drapery, floor, pillars, and stand. The Victoria and Albert Museum owns a similar picture, which appears to be in somewhat better condition, from which we might assume it was done at a later date and was perhaps even a copy. There are slight differences in the costume, the position of the model, and the head used for the figure.

The example of heraldic arms from Colonial Williamsburg that appears on page 19 is typical of eighteenth-century work. Tiny rolls form a sort of honeycomb background of light-colored vellum, parchment, or paper. On top of this

Paper filigree portrait. English. Undated. This portrait resembles, even to similar details on the gown, another wax model of Queen Anne wearing a court dress, which is dated about 1710. This may have been a later copy. Courtesy, Victoria and Albert Museum. Crown copyright.

17

background are mounted loops, scrolls, and curves of paper, also attached by their edge against the background. The design layer is gilded on the top edge and resembles gold filigree on a light background.

In the late eighteenth century, most of the English paper filigree work was done by ladies of leisure. They were taught by professionals in the art who also sold their own finished work. Patterns, mostly of swags, festoons, and other linear designs (similar to embroidery motifs), were published in *The New Lady's Magazine*, *Lady's Magazine*, and other eighteenth-and nineteenth-century women's magazines. Even Princess Elizabeth had a box and tea caddy and the filigree papers with which to work. It has been noted that a large number of tea caddies were being filigreed at that time. Tiny wax flowers, medallions, pictures, prints, and heraldic arms were surrounded by wreaths and framings of paper filigree. This paper work also adorned inkstands, trays, oval fire-screens, picture frames, small table tops, and even cribbage boards. Almost anything that could be decorated was probably attempted at this time, including a few larger pieces of furniture such as cabinets. And, of course, there were pictures, some of which may have been original and others that were probably made by following some of the patterns of the day.

Coat of arms. English. About 1750. The coat of arms is executed in bright red, blue, green, and gold against a tan background. The motto is black on a white ribbon. The border is made of flowing scrolls with an anchor in each corner. Courtesy, Colonial Williamsburg Foundation.

ASPERA
ET DURA PERFRINGIT
VIRTUS

19

QUILLWORK IN AMERICA

In the United States, most of the surviving quillwork pieces are sconces. These sconces are basically shadow box frames, with candle holders extending from the bottoms of the frames. All the sconces seem to have come from the Boston area, and they all have the same general design. A vase of quillwork holds a spray of flowers made of wax and wire. On either side are quilled birds. Sometimes there is a rooster on one side and a peacock on the other. Up and down the sides of the shadow boxes are very elaborate decorative trims of flowers, leaves, vines, or more birds—all done with bits of

Baskets of flowers, Lady Mary Lyon. England. c. 1810. Most of the flowers, stems, and leaves in this pair of baskets are done in paper work. Almost unnoticeable is the fact that both frames are covered with tiny paper rolls, through which wind vines with leaves and flowers, also of paper. When on display they are hung as a pair. Courtesy, Art Institute of Chicago.

rolled and fluted paper. F. C. Morse, in *Furniture of the Olden Time*, mentions a Mrs. Hiller, who in 1955 advertised herself as a teacher of quillwork and filigree along with other "gracious arts." Morse also describes a sconce made with paper of various colors, with the leaf, petal, and cone-shaped pieces gilded on one edge, coated with wax, and sprinkled with bits of glass to sparkle and glisten when the candles were lit.

Tea caddy. Probably English. c. 1790.
The "S" scrolls within the diamonds of
the latticework, as well as the larger
pieces, appear to have been rolled
around something of greater diameter
than the pin or pick used today. Each
section of this box has a border edge
of fluted paper. Courtesy, Tree Toys,
Hinsdale, Illinois.

"Hatchment" (the Foster coat of arms),
Lydia Foster Hutchinson. American.
1737. Courtesy, Museum of Fine Arts,
Boston, gift of Miss Lois Lilley Howe.

One of the most attractive sconces on display is also the smallest. It can be seen at the Metropolitan Museum of Art in New York. It is a single sconce with a black frame and is worked in blue paper with gilded edges.

Some of the best research and reporting on American quill-work, documenting the sconces and heraldic arms that have been produced in this country, has been done by Edith Gaines in various issues of *Antiques* magazine, as well as in a piece she wrote for *The Concise Encyclopedia of American Antiques*. By 1970 Mrs. Gaines had discovered and investigated twenty-eight sconces (twelve or possibly fourteen of them as pairs), four hatchments or coats of arms, two pictures (one of them, from Essex Institute, possibly being Continental rather than American), and one pair of wall cabinets.

A pair of sconces by Eunice Deering of Kittery, Maine, are probably the best known examples of American quillwork. They made use of the wax sheep that appear in a number of sconces, though not in all of them. One of these sconces has a pair of the peacocks and the other has a pair of the roosters.

Quillwork coat of arms. American, 1693. 17⅜ by 15¼ by 2⅝ inches. The initials of the Benjamin Smith family of Boston can be seen below the crest. This piece is particularly well preserved and contains quillwork on top of tiny scrolls in the crest, heavy leaves and plumes surrounding the crest, as well as the lighter flower border on the frame. Courtesy, The Henry Francis DuPont Winterthur Museum.

25

Picture of filigree or paper work. Origin unknown, possibly Continental European. This picture is done in red, blue and gold paper with gilded edges. The picture in the center appears to be a print of the *Virgin Mary and Christ Child*. The center basket and vases on either side are tilted forward at the top edge by means of a paper collar propping them to give a dimensional effect. Courtesy, Essex Institute, Salem, Massachusetts.

Paper work picture. United States. 1825-1860. 10½ by 8⁷⁄₁₆ by 2¹¹⁄₁₆ inches. This picture, made of wood, fabric, and fluted paper, is not quillwork, but it is a good example of the work being done at the end of the paperwork era. This may be of Pennsylvania Dutch or Germanic origin. Done in blue, yellow, cream, and green. Courtesy, The Henry Francis Du Pont Winterthur Museum.

The flowers in the various sconces all seem to have come from the same source, and the wax sheep appear to be all alike. This allows us to assume that there was a common source of instruction and supply. The differences between the various sconces, though noticeable, seem to be a matter of small preferences in design. The variation in sizes of the sconces may have been due to the cost of the materials or the amount of work that was necessary to create one of the pieces. The largest sconces measure 32 by 20¾ inches and the smallest is 17⅞ by 8¾ inches.

After the early nineteenth century, no notable works of paper filigree appeared; nor was there any apparent revival of interest in the craft through the first half of the twentieth century, except among the small number of researchers mentioned here. Appendix C lists all of the research that has appeared in the United States, except for material that has recently been published by commercial quilling companies.

Quill sconce. Quillwork plaque with attached brass candle sconces, multicolored, gilt, shells. Collections of Greenfield Village and the Henry Ford Museum.

Quillwork sconce, Eunice Deering. American. Eighteenth century. Courtesy, The Metropolitan Museum of Art, gift of Mrs. J. Insley Blair, 1948.

Quillwork sconce, Eunice Deering. American. Eighteenth century. Each of the sconces in this pair measures 30 by 14 inches. Courtesy, The Metropolitan Museum of Art, gift of Mrs. J. Insley Blair, 1948.

Upon hearing of quilling and rolling strips of paper on a pin, people frequently remark, "Oh, I learned *that* in school." Inevitably, what they remember learning was how to make beads by coiling long tapered strips of paper (1½ inches wide at one end and ¼ inch wide at the other), on a large needle. The roll is made from the wide end to the small end, producing a barrel-shaped hollow cylinder. The paper is then glued, shellacked, removed from the needle, and strung in a necklace. Perhaps these beads are a carryover from the old art of paper rolling.

About eighteen or nineteen years ago, Mrs. Margaret Carlson of Kansas City, Missouri, became acquainted with paper filigree when she received a request to do some repair and restorative work on some very old pieces. It was not long before she decided that if she could restore quilling she could also create her own pieces.

One of the projects Margaret Carlson undertook was that of covering a box with tiny coils. After edging the top and sides with narrow (¼-inch) strips of wood veneer and gluing on the

Rolled paper beads, Lura Silvernail. This is the form of rolled paper work most of us remember learning as children. The more colorful papers produce brighter beads. Old travel folders with their bright pictures are one good source for this paper.

Spanish Madonna, Margaret Carlson. A framework of long vertical cardboard strips is strengthened by cross pieces of shorter length cardboard. The quilled pieces are inserted and glued to these ribs. The head is from another small figure, and the hands are molded from a mixture of white glue and spackling compound. The figure is trimmed with small beads and gold braid, paint, and foil paper.

designs cut from cardboard, she added the coils to fill in the background area. When the glue was dry, she finished the box with a wood stain and liquid wax.

Margaret Carlson soon began teaching this rolled paper art, and people from many places in the country have learned quilling from her. They have carried away technique and inspiration to develop their own styles and adaptations of quilling.

More than ten years ago, Gini Antoine of Independence, Missouri, pioneered a delicate lacy form of paper filigree. She began the custom of naming the various coils when she first researched and introduced what she called a "lost art."

Quilling is just beginning its modern revival. New objects are being created all the time as more decorative uses are found for the art. The current revival is proof that the history of quillwork is still being written.

Chalk in eighteenth-century style,
Margaret Carlson. The flourish of this
type of design is particularly adaptable
to quilling and is one of the artist's fa-
vorite styles in which to work. The
simple, untrimmed frame allows the
elegant paper work to dominate.

Quilled box, Margaret Carlson. More
than 6,000 tiny coils were required to
cover the sides and top of this box,
which measures 6 by 5 by 5 inches.

2 Tools and Materials

Finding the right paper to produce a quilled design is of utmost importance. The choice of papers will depend on a number of factors: (1) what desired effects the finished product will have—whether you want a surface that looks massive and bulky, firm and compact, or delicate and airy; (2) to what use the quilling will be applied—whether the finished object will be handled frequently, as are quilled jewelry and free-hanging ornaments, handled less often, as on plaques or decorated vases, candle holders, frames and small boxes, or completely protected in a frame behind glass; and (3) your personal preference.

Quillers have used all varieties of paper. Some of the requisites of good paper for quilling are that it be heavy enough to hold its shape and not collapse limply when handled; that it be lightweight enough to roll smoothly and pliable enough when rolled without a tool; and that it be resilient enough to spring open to give the desired filigreed effect.

Another traditional requisite is that the strips of paper be

Papers come in many different weights, some of which are shown here. Moving clockwise from the lower left: a lightweight text paper, a lightweight cover stock, a heavy cover stock, a strip of watercolor paper. The difference in thickness of these papers is only slightly noticeable in a photograph, but the heavier papers require more pressure or tension to manipulate.

The same strips rolled into coils, with the lightest one at the bottom. This demonstrates how varying thickness affects the look of the finished project.

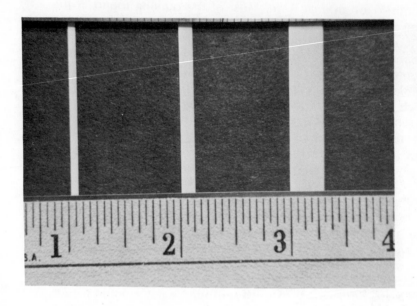

Variations in width. There is a difference in the "feel" of rolling the
strips of various widths. Changing
width may mean rolling a few extra
coils for practice.

Side view of coils. (Left to right) These
coils are made from paper ¼-inch
wide, ⅛-inch wide, and ¹/₁₆-inch wide.

about ⅛ of an inch wide. Most of the quilling found in the museums in the United States is done in paper of that width, although, on some of the decorated heraldic emblems, the paper looks a little wider and gives an effect of greater mass. Some quillers prefer to stay with the traditional ⅛-inch width, while others have experimented with paper as narrow as ¹⁄₁₆ inch or as wide as one inch. The various widths produce different effects. For example, a ¹⁄₁₆-inch-wide strip works well for use on gift enclosure cards, greeting cards, and small vases and boxes. Wider paper is often used for free-hanging ornaments, in framed decorative work, and on certain types of plaques. The ⅛-inch paper seems to be best for jewelry and will adapt most easily to general use.

In modern quilling, the choice of colors is broad and allows for a great deal of versatility in creating design. The early artisans were limited to handmade, heavy papers, probably in an off-white shade. The papers were colored with whatever natural stains or dyes were available, or they were gilded. By the sixteenth and seventeenth centuries, a few colored papers were available. When quilling was resurrected about eighteen years ago, the best papers available were in whites and pastel shades. As interest in quilling has grown, more kinds of papers have been used. People who quill are presently experimenting

Paper is available in almost any shade of a given color.

with all kinds of papers and finding ways to incorporate them in their work.

The growth of interest in quilling has led to the availability of quilling supplies, including paper precut to a relatively standard ⅛-inch width. It is well to note here that papers from different suppliers will differ somewhat in weight and that sometimes the weight of the paper will vary according to color, since desired colors are not always found in standard papers. Occasionally, the ⅛-inch width will vary a little from one manufacturer to another. You will want to experiment to discover your personal preferences as to weight, color, and width of paper.

Precut quilling paper is one of the least expensive materials for creative and rewarding design. Since most quilled pieces are made from strips two to eight inches long, a package of paper will go a long way. There is not much waste in the use of quilling paper. There is almost always a place to use the left-over pieces from a strip, either in a current design or a future

Chalk detail, Margaret Carlson. Seen close up from an angle, the layering and some variation in width of paper are apparent. Both factors add to the beauty of the finished design.

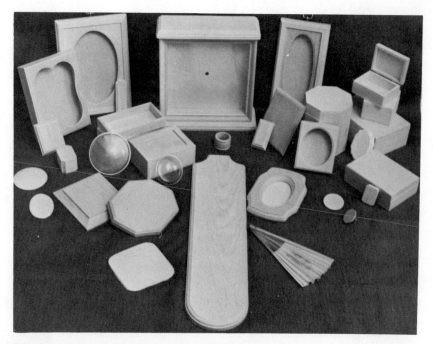

Display items. Many possibilities for display are found among boxes, plaques, domes, fans. Use your imagination to find unusual surfaces.

one. The most expensive part of the supplies used by quill artists is likely to be the frame, the plaque, or other background used to display the quilling.

Paper supplies are available in many craft shops across the country, and the number of shops is growing as quilling becomes more widely known. A number of companies carry an assortment of supplies, which they sell wholesale to craft shops and craft departments or which they retail to the general public. Many of these companies have put out instruction and pattern booklets, and some of them make kits. Quilling suppliers are listed in Appendix A.

Other craftsmen, who prefer to keep their work "pure," as well as people who want to keep the cost of supplies at a minimum will choose to select their own paper, cut it, sometimes color it themselves, and then proceed with the quillwork. Many of these people will also make their own display forms, as we will see in Chapter 5.

The advantages of preparing quilling paper by hand are the minimal expense, the opportunity to choose the exact width of the paper you want to use for your projects as well as the weight you prefer for rolling, and the possibility of discovering some unique and lovely colors, ready-made and home-dyed, to accent the work you do.

Advantages of machine-cut paper are the time and work saved in the cutting process, the less fuzzy look to the cut edges, and the bigger probability of having uniformly wide strips.

Cutting paper strips takes an extremely sure eye and steady hand. You must use a very sharp pair of scissors. Margaret Carlson cuts all of her own quilling paper and, although she usually works with paper about ¼ ·inch wide, narrower or wider strips add to the elegance of her work. The slightly wider paper on the outside swags of her framed chalk (shown on page 38), provide a more massive appearance, while the

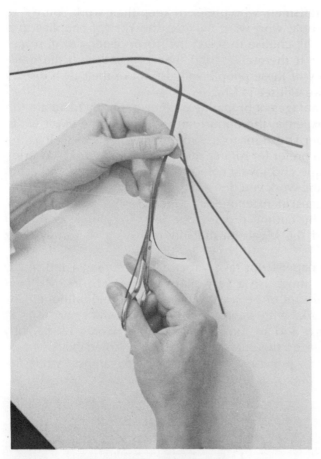

Cutting, stripping, and splitting require a pair of sharp scissors and careful attention.

Coloring your own paper with watercolors allows shading variations on one side as well as a different shade or color on each side.

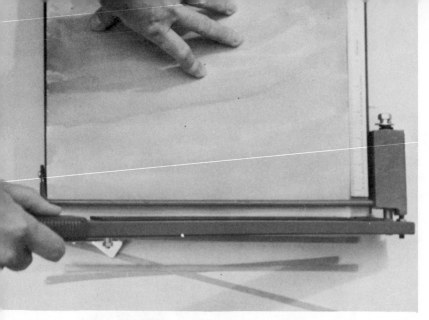

When using a paper cutter, hold the paper firmly and do not try to make the strips too narrow.

Stripping or splitting with a knife. A pane of glass, edges taped for safety, keeps the knife blade from dulling too quickly and allows easier guidance for a straight cut.

Flower plaque, Linda Bauer. Heavier watercolor paper cut into strips $^3/_{16}$ to $^5/_{16}$-inch wide gives a wood look to this quilling. Strip edges have been left white, accenting the coil.

Paper strip tree. The inventive Silvernails can keep their paper handy and separated when they demonstrate at craft fairs.

double layer in the wreath around the chalk provides a similar mass in a different manner.

An easier method of cutting paper is to use a home paper cutter. This limits the length of the strip you are able to cut to the length of the board (usually 12 or 18 inches). A sharp, new paper cutting blade will do a cleaner cut, but even then the edge of the cut may be fuzzy in appearance.

There are some limitations to the hand paper cutter. If the paper is very light, it is difficult to cut a straight piece that is less than a quarter of an inch wide. The paper tends to bend with the cutter, and the piece may be tapered or may not cut at all. Heavier papers with a little body will work better. You will need to do some experimenting with different kinds of paper.

Linda Bauer of Wheeling, Illinois, was impressed by the carved wood appearance of some very old quillwork she saw in Europe. She returned home and practiced duplicating that look with strips of rolled paper. She chooses water color paper and colors it with an inexpensive set of school water color paints. When both sides of a sheet are dry, Linda cuts the paper with a paper cutter into strips that may be as wide as $\frac{3}{16}$ of an inch, or even more. Sometimes she will color the cut edge of the paper to match the two sides, and at other times she will allow the white to show for an entirely different effect. Linda also makes her own plaques from scrap lumber and colors them to blend or contrast with her designs. Her pieces have a distinctive, massive wood appearance and contain many subtle shades of color.

When you use a narrow $\frac{1}{16}$-inch strip you may want to cut a standard $\frac{1}{8}$-inch strip in half. This process, called *stripping* or *splitting*, can be accomplished by using a pair of scissors or a sharp Exacto knife. Again, a sure eye and steady hand are necessary.

Easter egg in gingham, Alison Law, Hinsdale, Illinois. Photograph, Bob Anderson.

Dimensional flowers,
Lorraine Voss,
Birmingham, Michigan.
Photograph, Don Buckley.

45

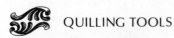

QUILLING TOOLS

Some people have a preference for one tool over another, and others prefer to use no tool at all. The important fact to notice is that different tools affect the finished appearance of the pieces in different ways.

Today, instead of the quill from a feather, a number of other tools have come into use. The first tool used by modern

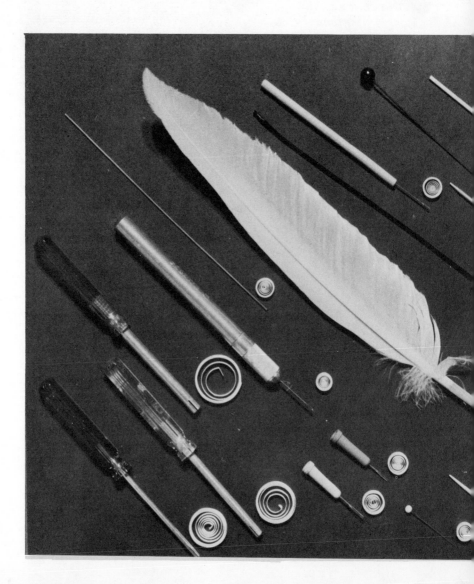

Quilling tools. At the tip of each tool is a coil made with it, illustrating the type of hole that appears in the center.

quillers was probably the hat pin or corsage pin. By far the biggest advantage of using the pin is that it enables the quiller to make a very tiny hole in the center of a quilled piece. The finer the pin, the smaller the hole, and the more delicate the appearance of the finished piece. Some people have even used a fine-gauge piano string wire around which to roll the paper. A long narrow pin, of whatever preference, is probably the most widely used of all the tools.

In Wichita, Kansas, the first quilling guild was formed more than a year ago. The members of this guild have discovered that a #3 insect pin is a very useful rolling tool. This pin is sturdy and long, and has a very tiny diameter. The quillers also use this pin for applying glue to the pieces as they work with their quilling. The pin is kept in a small square of wet sponge during the work session. The user applies only a very small drop of glue at one time, which keeps the glue from smearing on the tinier pieces. The sponge keeps the pin clean between applications and prevents awkward buildup of glue on the pin point.

Number 3 insect pin.

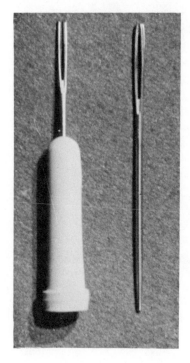

The needle at the right is a size 22 tapestry needle. On the left, the end of the needle eye has been filed off and sanded smooth. The point was inserted into a small tubular rubber cap and secured with a few drops of glue inside.

The next most popular tool is the round, tapered, wooden toothpick. It makes a slightly larger hole than the pin, and the hole is even larger if the pick is not thinly tapered or if the paper is rolled at the center instead of the end of the pick. The advantage to using the toothpick is that the rolling can be done more quickly. The wood pick helps grasp the paper, and the winding is done with the pick rather than with the fingers.

For more loosely coiled centers, the quilling can be done on larger darning needles, knitting needles, round pencils, and various sizes of dowels. Commercial tools for rolling metal strips produce the same results as these larger tools. Rolls made on larger tools will have a more hollow center and they have a somewhat limited use in design. They *do* have a quality of adding space to an entire quilling design, and the use of space in certain creative forms is as important as what fills that space.

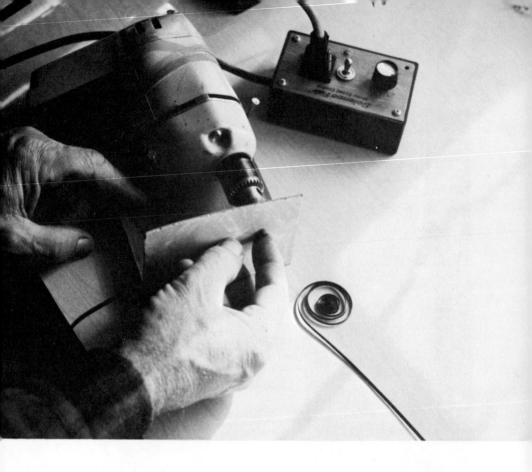

It is possible to make a tool that almost guarantees the user a smoothly rolled coil each time. It is a particularly helpful tool for people who have difficulty maintaining a steady light pressure or tension during the rolling. Such a tool can be made by grinding off the end of the long eye of a tapestry needle, about size #22. This leaves a slot into which the end of a paper strip can be inserted for rolling. Guy Silvernail, of Syracuse, New York, pushes the point of the needle into a wooden dowel about three inches long, which serves as a handle. An eraser or cork could fill the same purpose. However, when you use this tool, you may find that a small straight flap of paper cuts across the center hole. Furthermore, the center hole cannot be made as tiny as it can on the other end of the needle or on a pin.

Another method of rolling is that of using no tool at all. The paper is rolled entirely by hand. The center can be rolled

Coiling machine. This is Guy Silver-nail's answer to a question often heard from craft show patrons: "Why doesn't someone invent a machine to roll those coils faster?"

quite tightly when done this way, but some papers are harder to handle without squeezing them too tightly.

Sooner or later, as people watch others in the act of quilling, the question comes up about a tool to do all that rolling faster. What most people don't know, of course, is that the coiling goes along quite quickly and easily as the quiller becomes more adept through practice. The Silvernails have invented the ultimate in quilling tools: the automatic coil winder. A needle with the end of the eye cut off is secured in the end of a power drill bit holder. The drill is taped to a board with a baffle, which allows the needle to protrude just ⅛ inch outward. This exactly fits the width of the paper to be curled and assures a nice flat coil when the rolling is complete. The drill is also plugged into a transformer, which allows the user to regulate the speed of the turning drill and coil.

GLUES

Glue is another item essential to quilling. Some of the pieces need gluing to hold their shape, and all of the pieces are fastened together with small drops of glue in the formation of the design. For gluing the quilled pieces together, use a small drop of clear-drying white craft glue. The same type of glue is usually adequate for gluing the quilled design into place on a wood or cloth backing. For papers with a sheen, it is advisable to let the lighter glues jell for a short while or to use a heavier glue. The heavier clear-drying white glues hold better for gluing paper that has been sprayed with a metallic paint.

A different adhesive is necessary to hold a quilled piece to metal such as a pin back in making jewelry. A clear-drying household cement gives a stronger, more enduring bond in this instance.

USEFUL AIDS TO QUILLING

There are a number of items that can be very helpful when working on a quilling project. These are not as vital as the paper, tool, and glue, but they can ease the project of quilling.

A small pair of scissors is handy to have. Many people realize that tearing the paper strip allows the glued end to blend into the paper to which it is fastened, thus avoiding a blunt, jutting edge. However, in the center of the quilled piece, a trimmed edge will leave a smoother line and not have a fuzzy aspect.

A small plastic cup or bottle cap, into which only a few drops of glue are placed, will help keep the glue from drying out. Only a tiny amount of glue is used at a time, and a few drops will last through a work session.

To help achieve uniformity in the size of the pieces, use a ruler. A shorter strip of paper will coil into a smaller finished

Materials for quilling. Clockwise, starting at lower left: Styrofoam board covered with clear plastic, muffin tin, glue, glue cup and pick, damp sponge with #3 insect pin, straight pins, paper strips, tweezers, compass, scissors, large ruler, small ruler, protractor. In the center are a work surface of corrugated cardboard with grid covered by wax paper, and the following tools for rolling: quilling tool, hat pin, round toothpick, #3 insect pin.

piece. When a project takes a number of pieces of the same size, the ruler allows more accurate matching.

Almost everyone who quills finds a piece of wax paper taped onto a piece of corrugated cardboard to be a convenient work surface. The wax paper itself will easily peel off of a finished design if some glue gets off the strips onto the work surface. Also, wax paper is a cleaner surface, and the quilling does not pick up lint or colors. A graph, grid, or pattern can be slipped under the wax paper and fastened. The design can be assembled directly on top of the pattern and pinned into place as the pieces are glued together. Others prefer to work on a piece of styrofoam covered with a clear plastic wrap.

Two more handy items are tweezers and a muffin tin or divided plastic tray or box. The tweezers assist in picking up and placing the smaller pieces into position. The divided tin or tray will aid in keeping pieces separated according to size or shape.

Finally, it is helpful to keep a damp sponge, washcloth, or small commercial towelette at hand when working. This provides a convenient way to keep the fingers from getting sticky with glue and also lets the quiller moisten fingers or paper slightly, if necessary, when starting a coil.

When you begin to quill and are practicing rolling various coils, you might want to make a size chart for future reference. The pieces in the photograph on this page are made from strips of paper of lengths varying from 22 down to 2 inches. A chart of finished pieces, graduated in size, will en-

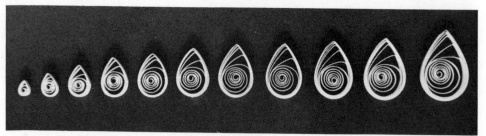

Size chart. These pieces are made from strips that are 22 inches down to 2 inches in length. Left to right, each one is 2 inches shorter than the one before it.

able you more easily to determine the approximate length of the paper strip you will need to fill a certain size space in your design. This chart may also be useful to you when you are trying to judge the approximate size of the finished work.

It is possible to standardize the sizes of the quilled pieces you make. The first determinant of the size of a rolled coil is the length of the paper used. The longer the strip of paper, the larger the coil. The second determinant is the amount of expansion of the coil that occurs. Paper that is rolled in a tight coil will stay more tightly coiled if it is held for a bit before releasing it. For closed coils, a jig can be made to accommodate coils of a certain length of paper. The jig consists of a ring of metal, plastic, or paper. When a coil is set into or passed through this jig, it expands only as far as the jig will allow. Then the end is glued to prevent further expansion. In this manner, you will be assured that all the coils slipped through the ring will be exactly the same size. This is particularly useful for creating geometrically perfect designs.

Using a coil jig.

Another aid to uniform geometric design is a grid, which can be drawn with the aid of a compass, protractor, and ruler. This grid consists of a series of concentric circles with the perimeters evenly spaced from each other. These circles are bisected by a number of lines, also evenly spaced to divide the circles into equal segments. Snowflake and six-pointed star patterns can be developed on this type of grid in order to avoid a haphazard-looking finished piece.

Another grid can be made by darkening some of the lines on a piece of graph paper. This grid is invaluable when you need straight lines for borders or right angle corners.

The pattern is also an aid to successful quilling. A pattern can be anything from a hand-drawn or photographed design, available commercially, to a simple outline that you take from a picture or draw yourself, to a free-form design that may have only a skeleton outline or collar as the pattern.

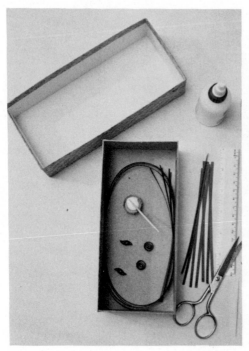

Travel kit. A small box (this one is 8 inches long, 3½ inches wide, 2 inches high) is all you need to carry a ruler, scissors, glue, bottle cap cup, paper strips, picks and pins for rolling and gluing. Add a plastic bag to hold the finished pieces and you are ready to leave.

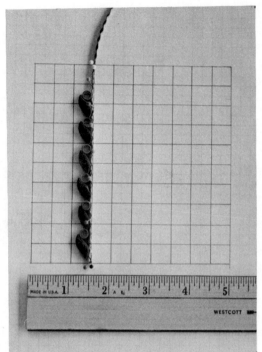

Line graph.

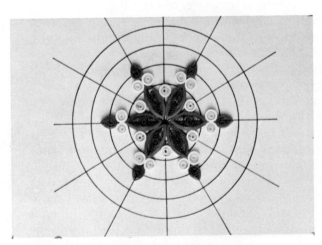

Round grid for geometric designs.

57

3 *Forming the Basic Shapes*

There are two essential processes involved in producing an item of quillwork. The first is making components that look attractive and do what you want them to do in a design. The second is originating, discovering, or planning the design itself. Both of these processes can be seen throughout this book in the artistic accomplishments, both simple and intricate, shared by those who quill.

As you learned in Chapter 2, there are three basic materials you need when learning to quill: paper strips, a tool on which to roll the paper, and glue. Once you have these items, you are ready to begin. Wash your hands before you start—otherwise the paper will become shabby and lose its crisp look because of the accumulation of oil and dirt from your fingers. Keeping your fingers free of glue is also important for ease in handling the pieces, especially the small ones.

You will soon discover that there is only one basic step to learn—rolling the coils. And the only way to master rolling is to do it. You must maintain a certain tension that allows the

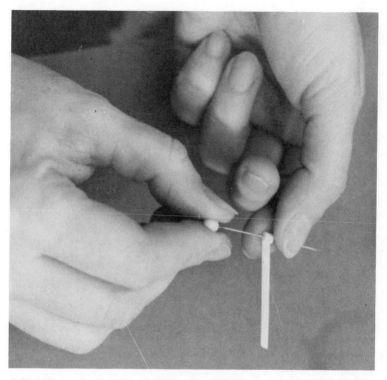

ROLLING THE COIL ON A PIN. Roll the coil between your fingers with a firm, even hold. The pin does not turn but acts as an axis to brace the paper.

coils to spring free, smoothly and evenly. Developing a "feel" for this tension comes only with practice. The look of even coils contributes much of the beauty to quilling.

There is no right or wrong way to roll a coil—different people can achieve similar results with different methods. By the time you have made a few of each of the coils pictured here,

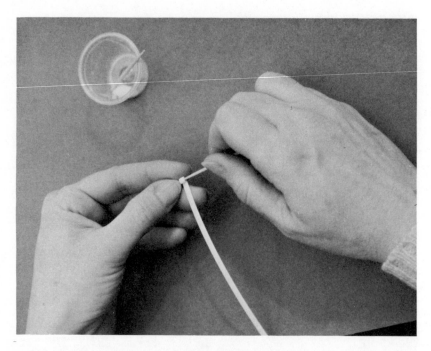

ROLLING ON A TOOTHPICK. Squeeze tight enough to turn the pick and roll paper with it for about two turns. With practice, you can use the pick to carry the paper as you rotate the pick toward you with your right hand. Hold the paper between the fingers of your left hand just tight enough to keep the coil from slipping.

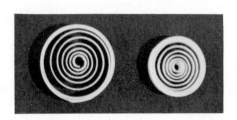

you will be well on your way to mastering the rolling process. To help you, here are a few tips for achieving more consistent results.

1. If you are rolling on a pin or a toothpick, or on any tool with a fairly small diameter, it is a good idea to wrap the paper very tight for the first couple of rolls. This makes the rolling easier and, on a toothpick, allows the pick to carry the paper as you roll.

2. Be sure to maintain tension throughout the rolling process so that the center of the coil does not begin to unwind before the whole coil is wound. Maintaining tension keeps the coil more even and smooth.

3. If you have difficulty in starting the coil on a pin or a toothpick, dampening your fingertips slightly will help. You might also moisten the end of the paper a little.

4. If the coils look bent, mashed, or uneven, you may be squeezing too hard as you roll. Try loosening the tension slightly.

5. If the coils do not spring free smoothly or open as wide as you want them to, you probably have placed too much tension on the paper.

6. If you control the way the coil springs free, you can maintain a more even look and vary the size and appearance of the finished coil.

Two types of coils are used in quilling. The *open coil* is usually not glued until it is put into a design, except to hold

Each of these coils is made from a strip of paper 11½ inches long. The coil on the left was allowed to expand almost to full capacity and thus has a lacier look. The coil on the right was allowed to expand only part way and has a heavier edge, which gives it a mosaic quality.

the coil in a precise position or shape. A *closed coil,* on the other hand, must be glued shut so that it will remain a standard size. The closed coil is made by rolling all the way from one end of the strip of paper to the other and gluing the outside end. The open coil can be rolled fully or partially from one end or both ends. It is left unglued.

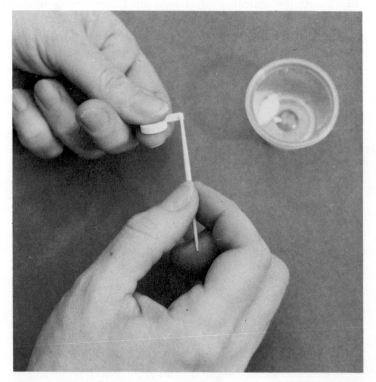

GLUING A CLOSED COIL. When the coil is the desired size, place a small drop of glue right at the end of the strip. Always glue closed coils before pinching them into other shapes.

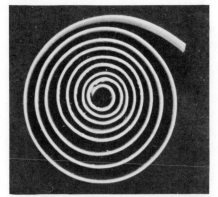

LOOSE, OPEN COIL. Roll from only one end; then let the coil spring loose. This small spring is used as filler when the design calls for an open space to be occupied. This coil is also known as an open scroll.

SCROLL. Roll from both ends of the strip on the same side of the paper. The two coils meet in the middle.

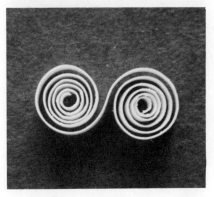

"S" SHAPE. Roll from both ends of the strip on opposite sides of the paper. The "S" can also be shaped into a question mark.

63

TENDRIL. Roll in a spiral shape on a pin or a pick, or twist into a spiral as tight as desired. The tendril is also called a spiral, rope, or twist.

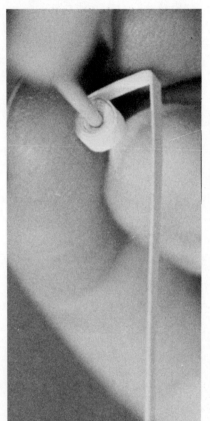

OPEN HEART. Fold the strip of paper in half and roll the ends in toward the center of the crease.

 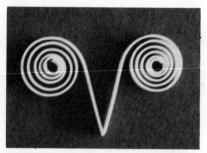

QUOTES. Fold the strip of paper in half, as for the heart and "V," but roll the ends in the same direction. One coil will be rolled toward the center crease and the other away from it.

"V" SHAPE. Fold the strip of paper in half as for the heart, but roll the ends on the outside of the paper, away from the inner crease.

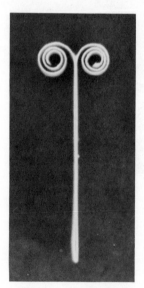

FEELERS. Roll only a small part of the paper strip, leaving the rest of the strip straight. Feelers can be made on one paper strip or on a folded strip as in the "V" shape.

PEG. To make a peg, roll a strip of paper tight from one end to the other and glue the end while the coil is still tight. Pegs can be used in designs themselves or glued to the underside of a design to raise the design just enough to accent the lacy pattern and add dimension to the finished product.

CONTOURED PEG. After rolling and gluing a tight coil, push the peg up from underneath the center to contour its shape. This adds another element of dimension to the quillwork.

Mushrooms, students of Hope Lutheran School, Chicago, Illinois. Quilling strips were cut from sheets of colored paper, glued together at the ends, and wrapped into large rolls. These rolls were pressed into shapes of mushroom tops and stems. For permanence, a clear glue was applied to finished pieces. Much larger pieces can be made using this technique with wider strips of paper. Photograph, Emil Becker.

Contoured medallion, Betty Christy.

CONE. A third element of dimension can be achieved with a tight coil pushed into a cone shape. In very old quillwork, the cone was used extensively to add relief. To achieve the sharper point of the cone, you must wind the paper from the beginning in a tight spiral fashion. The piece is glued while it is still rolled tight. Like contoured pegs, cones must be handled gently unless they are sealed in their shapes with a coating of glue or heavy lacquer. They flatten easily and are difficult to coax back into place with the same even look. Worse yet, the center might pop out, and it can never be put back.

Layers of quilling add contouring to this red and white medallion. The shapes are raised on pegs.

LOOSE COIL. Roll a strip of paper into a tight coil and, before gluing the end, let the coil spring or expand. If you control the coil as it expands, you can let it expand fully for a more lacy and delicate look; or you can stop the expansion and achieve an appearance of mosaic with a heavier looking edge or rim.

Pendant, Elsie Grammer, Chicago, Illinois. An inexpensive gold colored bracelet from the dime store borders this geometric design of orange, yellow, and white pieces and makes a solid rim for hanging as a medallion.

PEACOCK EYE. This shape, also known as a raindrop or teardrop, is formed by pinching a loose coil on one side. Variations can be achieved by the method used in pinching. The coil can be short and fat, or long and thin. The center can be pulled down to the point or allowed to be in the wider end. If the coil is pinched so that the glued end of the strip is near the point, the ridge will be minimized.

PETAL. To make this shape, bend the tip of the peacock eye slightly to one side.

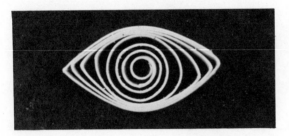

DIAMOND. By pinching the opposite sides of a round, loose coil, you can make a diamond, also called a marquise or an eye-shaped coil. The diamond must be pinched carefully to keep the center located in the wider center section and to shape it evenly.

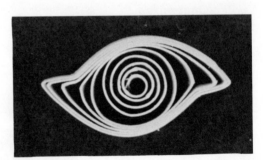

LEAF SHAPE. By bending one or both ends of the diamond, you can produce a leaf shape.

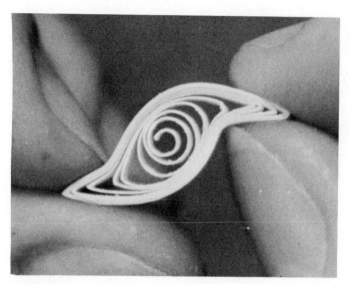

Bending a leaf shape.

OVAL. Squeeze a loose coil into an oval shape, but do not point the ends as you would to make the diamond.

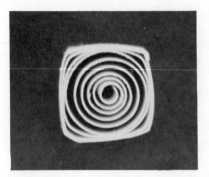

SQUARE. Roll a loose coil and form a diamond. Then pinch the sides into points, forming the square.

RECTANGLE. Squeeze the round, loose coil into an oval and pinch two corners at each end.

Tropical fish, Linda Bauer. Oranges, yellows, browns, and black provide a vivid contrast.

STAR or HOLLY LEAF. Form a diamond; then pinch the side points by pushing together from the end points. This puts more bend in the sides than occurs in the square shape. Variation and unevenness are often desired for this piece.

Pinching a holly leaf.

TRIANGLE. Pinch the outer edge of a loose coil into a three-sided shape. Most of these pieces look better if the centers are kept as round as possible.

HALF MOON. Pinch a loose coil so that it has two points, with an indentation on one side of the coil.

CLOSED HEART. Pinch a triangle and indent one side.

TULIP. A shape similar to the half moon, but with an extra point in the center.

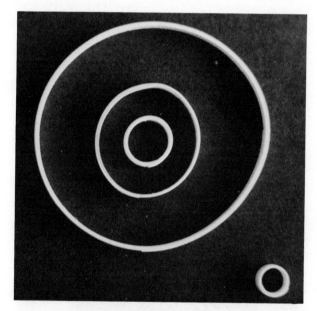

CIRCLE. Wind the paper strip around forms of varying diameters as many times as desired; glue. Dowels, pill bottles, and coins all make good jigs for making even circles.

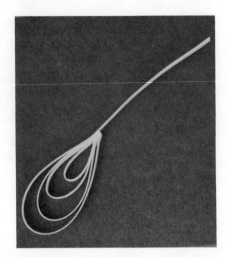

WHEAT. Make a small loop at the end of a strip of paper and glue. Continue the strip around in a slightly larger loop and .glue at the point again. Repeat this process until you have a series of loops all glued at the point. These can be pinched at the other end or left rounded.

A butterfly made from circles.

Butterfly, Sally Mann, Milwaukee, Wisconsin. This design makes use of the wheat shape.

More circles used as a frame.

VARIATION 1. Fold a strip of paper in half and crease firmly. Start rolling at the open end and roll the two ends of the strip together at the same time. As you roll, the inner strip, which has a tendency to buckle, forms a tighter coil, and curves into a graceful arch.

VARIATION 2. Fold a strip of paper in half and crease firmly. Roll the double strip from the folded end about halfway down the length. Roll the open ends as you would for a "V" shape.

VARIATION 3. Fold a strip of paper in half and crease firmly. Fold each end of the strip into the middle and fasten with a small drop of glue. Roll in the folded ends toward the inside of the crease. As you roll, the inner paper will curve into a graceful arch and the resulting piece will form an unusual heart shape.

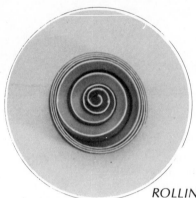

*ROLLING TWO COLORS TOGETHER.
Two different colors of paper can be
rolled at the same time, producing one
appearance when the lighter shade is
on the outside and another when the
darker shade is on the outside. This is
an effective technique to use when
delicate shadings are desired in a
finished design.*

*TWO COLORS END TO
END. Glue two or more
strips of color end to end
and roll one larger coil.
Begin rolling with the
color you wish to appear
in the center of the coil.*

82

Butterfly, June M. Hargis, Deerfield, Illinois. This design uses two colors of paper rolled together.

Basket, Patricia Sova.

83

Plaque, June M. Hargis.

Picture, Diane Cunningham, Hinsdale, Illinois.

"Coltsfoot Flower," Lura Silvernail. The center is made of 1½-inch strips rolled into tight coils. The petals are composed of 1¾-inch strips and 1½-inch strips folded in half in groups of four or five, cut almost to the fold. The leaves are 17- and 9-inch strips rolled into loose coils and pinched.

Paper bow.

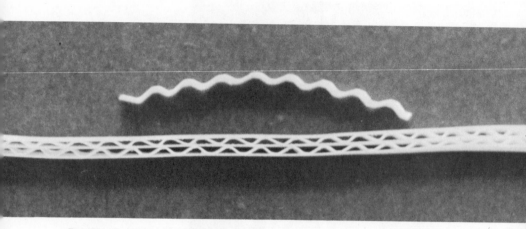

FLUTING. Strips folded in small pleats by hand were often used in very early quillwork and still add interest and beauty today. The fluted strip in the top of this photo can be glued between flat strips, as shown. This arrangement was used to decorate many of the old sconces.

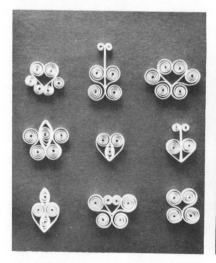
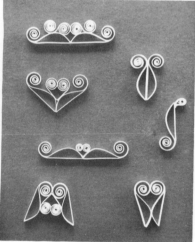

FLUTING WITH A DRILL. An easy way to flute paper is to run a strip through the gears of a clean hand drill. It helps to have an assistant guide the paper.

CLUSTERS. Various pieces can be combined in pairs or clusters of more than two into very unusual designs. Sometimes these designs, repeated, can form the pattern for a border. At other times they can be a separate grouping in the corner of a picture. There are probably thousands of combinations that can be used—some are pictured here to start you thinking on your own.

87

4 *A Simple Lesson*

      This chapter will take you through one simple project and offer some ideas on what to do with your first design.

      For one daisy you will need three or four strips of white quilling paper, one strip of yellow, and one strip of green. Put a few drops of glue in a glue cup. Use a pick or a pin for rolling, and work on a sheet of waxed paper. If you have practiced making the coils in Chapter 3, skip the next paragraph—you are probably already turning out fairly even quilled pieces and you have a pretty good idea of your preference for a tool.

      If you have never quilled before, you will need about six to ten additional strips of white paper for practice. Tear about five of the strips into pieces about 5½ inches long. Read Chapter 3 to learn *how* to roll. Choose a tool for rolling—a round, wooden, tapered toothpick will probably be the easiest to start with—and use the strips you have torn into quarter lengths for practicing. The coils you will need to know for the daisy are all closed coils: the loose coil, the peacock eye (or teardrop), and the leaf shape.

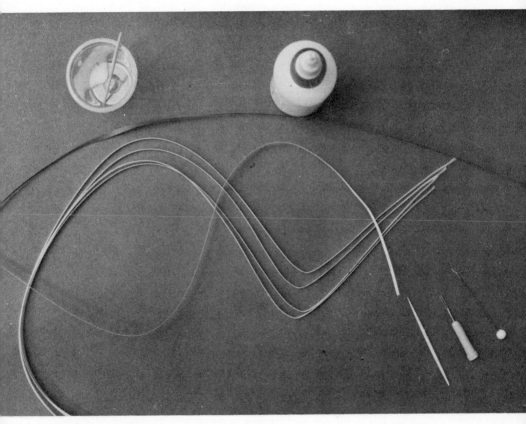

Materials for daisy.

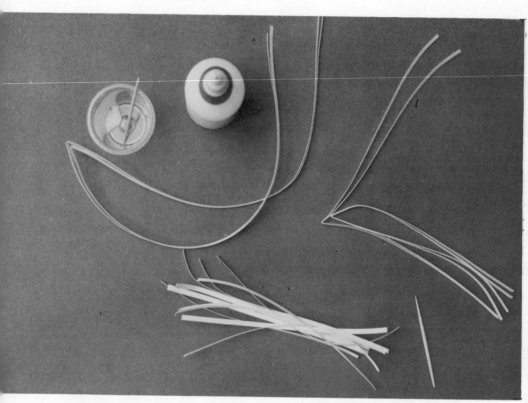

Practice paper.

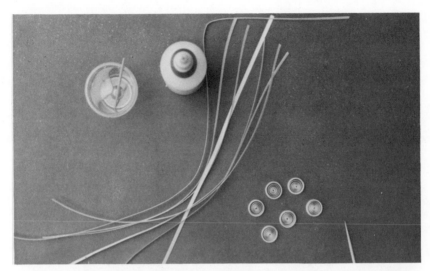

1. When you are ready to begin the daisy, tear three of the full-length white strips in half and make six loose coils with these pieces. The loose coils should all be the same size. (You may need to make two or more extra coils from the spare strips in order to get six of the same size.) It is easier to match round coils for size before the shape is changed.

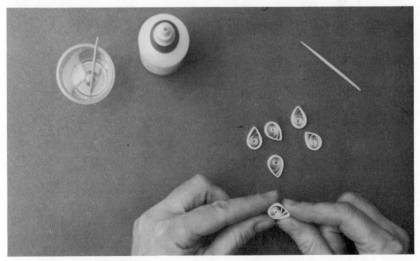

2. When you are satisfied with the matching coils, pinch them into peacock eyes.

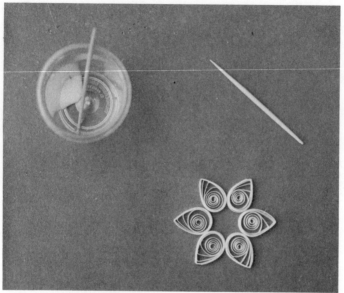

3. Place the peacock eyes in a circle, with the points heading out. Place them close enough together so that each rounded side touches the coil next to it.

4. Make one loose coil from a half strip of yellow paper. Before you glue the end, make sure that it has expanded just enough to fill the center space formed by the six white peacock eyes.

5. Arrange the white pieces around the yellow center so that each white piece touches the center and the neighboring pieces. Be sure that the points head straight out so that opposite points are in a straight line. Also check to see that the paper lines in the points of the peacock eyes all swing in the same direction.

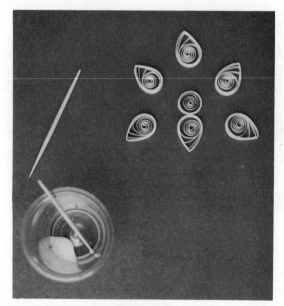

6. Put a small drop of white, clear-drying glue at every point where the coils touch each other. Start by gluing one peacock eye at its rounded base to the center piece.

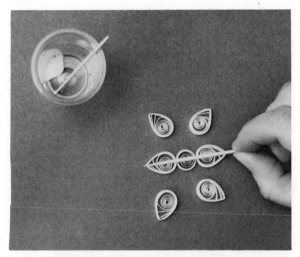

7. Glue the opposite peacock eye in the same manner to the other side of the yellow center, keeping the points aligned.

8. Glue the other four peacock eyes with a drop of glue at each point where they touch each other and the center, lining up the opposite points.

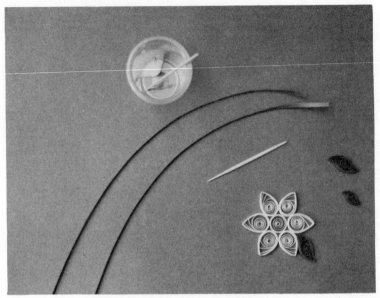

9. Tear the green strip in half and make two leaf shapes. If you want to make one leaf a smaller size, use a quarter-length strip of green.

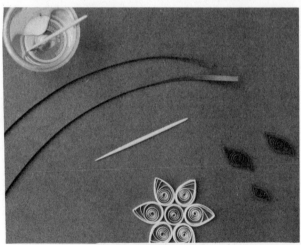

10. Fit the first leaf shape between two of the petals and glue on points of contact.

11. Fit the second leaf shape beside the first, and glue where the pieces touch.

12. After the glue has dried for a few moments, the daisy can be lifted off the wax paper, placed on a newspaper, and sprayed with a clear acrylic or plastic sealer. Spray lightly two or three times on each side. Now your daisy is ready to be put to some use.

VARYING THE DAISY SIZE

If you want to make smaller daisies, use strips of paper half as long as the ones you used in the lesson. To make a very large daisy, use a full strip of paper (usually about 23 inches long) for the petals, leaves, and center.

The daisy in four sizes.

Daisy pin.

Earrings.

99

Frame trim.

Recipe box.

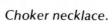

Ring.

Choker necklace.

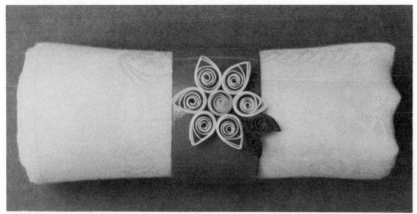

Napkin ring.

Place card.

Plaque.

Barrette.

5 *Enhancing and Displaying Quilling*

There are many ingenious processes that you can experiment with to make each piece of your quillwork unique.

 ADDING COLOR

In addition to using prepared colored paper, you might want to investigate the effects that you can achieve by using color applied to white paper, either before or after rolling the pieces for a design.

One possibility is using watercolor paints, as we described in Chapter 2. Apply the color to the paper before cutting it into strips. Another way to add color to paper is to mix a dye with water in a large 9- by 13-inch glass baking dish. Place a few strips at a time in this solution and allow them to stay until the desired shade is achieved but not so long that the paper falls apart—ten minutes is probably safe. Then carefully place the paper strips flat on a newspaper to dry thoroughly. They will roll just as well as before, and the color will be your own. Some of the most unusual shades of antique rosy beige can be obtained from spicy teas that are brewed just as directed on the package. Coffee is another unusual shade. Grape juice, allowed to reach varying intensities, makes an extraordinary color mixture for a quilled grape cluster. Vegetable dyes will produce most of the other hues, and you can acquire shades from pale to intense in all of these.

White paper strips can be tacked onto a heavy piece of cardboard with straight pins and sprayed, first on one side and then on the other, with any shade of paint available in a spray can. Gold, silver, and other metallic sprays used in this manner produce a finished coil that resembles a metal strip that has been rolled.

Spraying paper gold.

Gilding the edges of paper.

Gilding the edges of the paper can also be done before rolling strips into various coils. This is most easily accomplished using the paper strips that are available commercially. If a pack of thirty-five to fifty white strips is stretched on edge tightly between two boards (buttressed by something heavy such as bricks), the top edge can be sprayed with gold or other metallic paint. After this coating is dry, the strips will have a very even edging of gilt.

Another way to add color to a piece of quillwork is to do it after the design is complete. Gold spray paint, sprayed lightly, gives an ordinary simple design a look of antique elegance. Spray the design with a paper sealer first to prevent the color from bleeding. Then spray with a light coat of gold. Again, any color can be used and the effect varies with the amount of paint used.

Parakeet, Linda Bauer. The watercolor paper is painted in shades of blue and green.

Resin palette, Sally Mann, Milwaukee, Wisconsin. The quilled design is set in the resin, to which color is added for the third layer.

105

For hundreds of years, gold leaf has been used in gilding. If you want to use it, you must first use a special sizing compound as an adhesive and then roll the gold leaf on or apply it with a brush. The next step is pouncing or burnishing. There seems to be no record of how so much gilding was done on the quillwork of a few centuries ago. However, today we have gold paints (actually, they are made of bronze, because gold is so costly) and gilding is much easier. If you want to gild the edges of part or all of your finished design, you can roll on the gold paint with a cotton swab or apply it with a small paintbrush.

Deep antique shadow box table with poppies. © *Betty Nelson, Arlington, Texas. Photograph, Don Buckley.*

Basket of flowers, © *Betty Nelson. A layer of quilled pieces adds to the texture of this basket. The velour leaves form a visible layer beneath the flowers, and the top layers of petals are pulled forward for another approach to dimension. Courtesy, Quilling Bee Enterprises, Arlington, Texas.*

JEWELS

Various jewels can be combined with quilling to add sparkle or a touch of richness. Tiny gold balls, seed pearls, or sparkling stones can be attached with a little drop of clear-drying glue.

Flower spray with pearls, Lora Porter.
Tiny seed pearls decorate the flowers
and the arrangement is tied together
with a rope of pearls.

Three-dimensional cross, Lora M. Porter, Wichita, Kansas. The framework of this cross is done in ⅛-inch-wide strips of paper and the panels in between are done with ¹⁄₁₆-inch-wide strips, which contribute another dimension and a look of delicacy to the design.

Flowers with beaded stems, Sally Mann, Milwaukee, Wisconsin.

 DIMENSION

Adding dimension is one way to add life to quilled pictures. Dimension can change the flat, carved-fretwork look to one of more action. Dimension can also assist in making quillwork more realistic. One of the artistic pleasures and challenges of working with quilled pieces is that of reproducing the real life item as closely as possible in the mosaic style.

Dimension can be achieved in a number of different ways. One method is the use of the peg, discussed in Chapter 3, to raise the design up from the background. A second way, that of building your design on a wider collar, will be discussed in Chapter 6.

An interesting touch of dimension can be added by turning some of the pieces onto the flat side and letting them reach out toward the viewer.

Simple layering is exactly that: making a bottom layer and then making a second layer to glue on top of it.

It is possible to add dimension by inserting extra pieces at various angles and by adding small amounts of other materials for contrast.

Another way to introduce dimension in a picture, without

Details of mushroom. The form was made with a plastic mold.

Basket purse, Arlene Spriggs Trujillo. Mushrooms trim this basket purse. Velvet leaves, cord, and hardware are added as further decoration. Courtesy, International Leisure Activities, Inc. Photograph, Arthur C. Frocke.

using layering, is to raise the components of a design by using a silicone glue to bring the pieces forward. This method allows variation in depth of layers for a more individual style of design.

One handy way to achieve dimension is to use a form or mold to which the quilled coils can be glued. The mold will allow the quilled form to keep its shape without caving in. Molds are available in a large assortment of forms.

Single flower, Juanita Rains.

Detail of the table on page 106. Notice how the flowers are raised to add dimension.

"Miss Priss," a poodle by Dixie Miller and Rose Ann Sloan. © *Quaint Quilling.*

113

Ornament, Linda Bauer. Linda creates this ornament in three major steps: *(1) She makes an eight-pointed design on her work board (the portion facing, in the photo); (2) She builds up on top of that design (the cross sections that we see); (3) She makes another section identical to that in Step 2, which she can then glue to the other side of the first section.*

EMBEDDING QUILLING IN PLASTIC

One of the ways to preserve and display your quilling is to embed the finished design in plastic, to be used as a paperweight or mounted on a bookend frame.

Choose the size and shape of mold that is best for your purpose, and pick the resin and catalyst you wish to use. Then quill up your design. You may choose a free-form style or a geometric design, or you may follow a pattern.

Mix the resin and catalyst for the first layer according to di-

Paperweight, D. Tracy. The layered quilling is yellow and orange with green at the bottom. The glass magnifies the quillwork.

rections and pour into the mold. When this layer has set, put in your quilled design (*top side down* because you are working in reverse) and pour the second layer of resin just to cover. The third layer can remain clear or can have color added for an opaque contrasting background. When you remove the cured plastic from the mold, the bottom will become the top of the finished piece.

 GLASS PAPERWEIGHTS

Available in many craft shops are glass paperweights that are hollowed to allow a three-dimensional item to fit inside. With a little experimenting, it is possible to fasten flat or layered designs onto a covered or painted backing and glue the design to the paperweight so that the quilling is inside.

Paperweight, Mabel Waller.

Clock, Barbara Maddox. A number of ways to achieve dimension have been used in this quillwork clock. Pegs have been used for raising the level of some of the flowers. A partial third layer of flowers is glued directly to the second layer. Barbara has used 3- and 4-inch strips of white and yellow for the daisy petals, 1-inch strips for the centers, and 2-, 3-, and 4-inch strips of gold and yellow for the pressed heart flowers. The leaves are made of 2½-inch strips of olive green and light green. The background is burlap cloth applied with paste used for fabric wallpaper. Courtesy, Quill Art, Ballwin, Missouri.

117

MOUNTING QUILLWORK

There are a number of other unusual ways for displaying your quillwork. You can put your quilling on a wooden plaque that has been painted with an enamel or stained to let the wood grain show. Anything that can be mounted on a plaque can also decorate the cover of a box. However, you must remember that these coils and designs are always exposed to air, dust, and dirt. It is wise to spray the finished plaques or boxes with a few coats of clear plastic or acrylic spray. This lets you feather dust the pieces or even wipe them with a slightly damp cotton swab.

Gilded, jeweled Victorian fan. Priceless Pastimes Art Co. Ltd., specializing in paper quilling materials. Virginia G. Antoine, 12101 Newbury Lane, Independence, Missouri 64052.

Elephant, Doris E. Knighton, Spring Hill, Florida. The outline of this little elephant was copied from a child's coloring book and neatly filled in with tiny quilled pieces. The elephant is not much bigger than 2½ by 3½ inches. It is mounted on a plaque.

"The Water Can," Lora Porter and Eloise Basinger, Wichita, Kansas.

Antique watch, B. Christy. This antique watch face has been mounted on a dark blue velvet background. The finished border and corner clusters were sprayed with a paper sealer first and then with gold to give the aged look. Photograph, Bob Anderson.

Clown, Joyce Zivic. Courtesy, JDJ Designs, Manchester, Missouri.

120

Cameo on plastic dome, B. Christy.
The shaded rosy beige of the cameo
matches the tea-dyed simple heart and
peacock eye border. They are enhanced by the cream-colored dome.

Box, embedment, B. Christy. The
cameo and quilling in this recessed
box lid are covered with Envirotex to
protect the coils.

*Apples, Joyce Zivic. Courtesy, JDJ
Designs, Manchester, Missouri.*

*Flowers, Mabel Waller, Oak Park, Illinois. Three of these flowers are made
of scrolls that have been placed on
their back across each other and centered by a tight coil.*

122

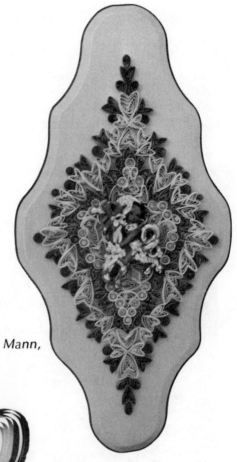

Plaque with terra cotta, Sally Mann, Milwaukee, Wisconsin.

Butterfly, Sally Mann,

MAKE YOUR OWN EASEL

For a change from hanging all your quilled plaques on the wall, a very handy little stand can be made from a self-pleating type of drapery hook. The hook needs to have at least four pleating prongs. The center two prongs are bent up to hold the plaque or fan, and the hook itself is bent back to form the easel leg for support. (The metal material clamp at the top end of your new stand can be pried off fairly easily.)

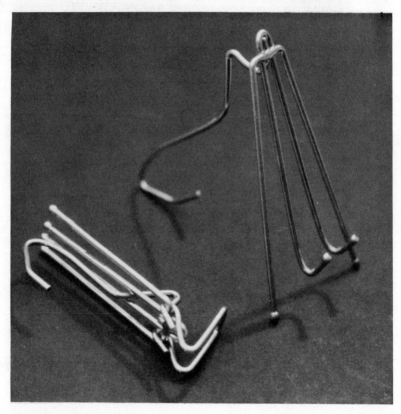

Drapery pleater easel.

 PROTECTIVE ENCLOSURES

In order to give quilling the best protection, make a shadow box frame with a glass to seal out the dirt. The backing you use is a matter of choice. Quilling shows off to best advantage on a plain fabric or paper, although you will notice that some of the quillwork in this book has been successfully applied to

"Double Cornucopia," Margaret Carlson.

Flower basket, quilling design by Betty Meisenbach, from Concepts in Quilling, *published by Cunningham Art Products. The flowers are done in bold modern color, and the unusual treatment of the coils conveys the sense of a handwoven basket.*

small patterned fabric or paper. Some of the backings you can use are burlap, velour paper, construction paper, wood, velveteen, velvet, silk, gingham, textured papers, and wallpaper.

If you want to make your own frame, Margaret Carlson has an unusual and inexpensive method. She finds a sturdy cardboard box with a cover that completely surrounds the top and sides (such as a box for a dress or suit). She reverses the box, fitting it inside the cover and gluing it securely all around the sides and back. Then she lines the box with a fabric or damask wallpaper. She glues her finished quillwork onto the backing and fits a thin pane of glass over the entire double-edged front opening and fastens the pane securely. Finally, she covers the outside of the box with a suitable fabric or paper and frames the edge of the glass with gilt paper or braid.

One of the most elegant mats for quillwork is velvet or velveteen. No matter what color you choose for the background, a finished piece of quillwork seems to become even more beautiful when mounted on this soft, plush material.

Daisies, Sally Mann, Milwaukee, Wisconsin. These daisies are elevated at various levels, with the green leaves placed directly on the red velour background.

127

In an instruction portfolio, Berny Umland of Albuquerque, New Mexico, has provided a useful description of matting and framing under glass:

Since the quilling adds a dimension of at least ⅛ inch, it is necessary to have a shadow box frame. The molding at the back of the frame must be at least ½-inch deep, and preferably ¾-inch deep, in order to have room for ⅛-inch thickness of glass, ⅛ inch for the velveteen mat and ⅛ inch to ¼ inch for the quilling. The glass also magnifies finger prints, dust, or paper crumbs; so be sure to check your assembly several times before sealing.

For mounting, you will need a velveteen-covered mat. Cut a piece of thin cardboard ⅛ inch shorter and ⅛ inch narrower than the opening in the frame. For instance, the mat for an 8 x 10 picture is cut 7⅞ inches by 9⅞ inches, the amount of space needed for your velveteen. Cut the fabric at least ½ inch larger all around than the cardboard. Center the cardboard and then cut off the *corners* of the fabric, flush with the cardboard. Run a thin line of white glue on the velveteen and fasten to the cardboard. You should have neat corners with no extra bulk.

Now you are ready to mount your design. Inspect it carefully for excess glue. Remove with tweezers, forceps, or scissors. Inspect your mat—brush off any threads or dust. A small piece of masking tape cleans it neatly. Center the quilled design and glue in place with a tiny dab of glue on a toothpick placed under the densest part of the pattern. Four or five dabs should hold it in place.

Make your boxing by cutting strips of corrugated cardboard or mat board ³⁄₁₆ inch to ½ inch wide. Cover each strip with velveteen.

Now clean the glass and glue in your strips. Put the mat in place and check for dust or fingerprints. When you are satisfied, tape mat in place with masking tape or gummed paper tape. Cover the back with wallpaper or brown craft paper and add a hanger.

In her instructions, Berny Umland also informs us that four or five coats of Deft, thinned one-half with lacquer thinner, gives an ivory-like finish to white paper quillwork.

In Chapter 6 you will find many other ideas for displaying and mounting your quillwork projects.

Flower panel, Bernice T. Umland. The very unusual style of quilling takes on the look of a pen and ink drawing when mounted on black velvet. The lacy forms are fine and graceful. To retain symmetry, the artist recommends cutting strips of paper for identical parts (leaves, for example) in the same lengths. Courtesy, Mrs. George Best.

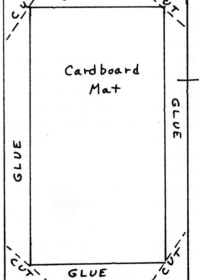

Family tree, Barbara Maddox. Barbara rounds out her family tree with extra pieces inserted after the first two layers are completed. Courtesy, Quill Art, Ballwin, Missouri.

"An Apple A Day," Betty Thompson. This mold was created by cutting a styrofoam ball in half and painting it red before adding the red coils. A teardrop jewel adds a highlight to the apple, and seed-pearl-centered blossoms finish the picture.

Brooch, Betty Thompson, Wichita, Kansas. A beautiful old silver jeweled brooch serves as a focal point for this quilled framework. The grey paper is edged with silver and the shadow box frame is matching antique silver. The velvet background is a dusky ˙blue to blend with the whole piece.

Eighteenth-century lady, Lora Porter and Eloise Basinger. This is an unusual combination of quillwork with an elevation (a picture done in layers).

131

"Grandfather Clock," Dixie Miller and Rose Ann Sloan. © Quaint Quilling.

Quilling with bread dough flowers, Lora Porter.

132

Design, Alice Yahn. This very intricate work is done in many symmetrical layers.

Monarch butterfly, Frank Tracy. The orange, yellow, and brown butterfly appears about to take off from his burlap perch. Pegs glued under the outside edges of the wings raise them from the background. Photograph, Bob Anderson.

133

6 *Creating Quilling Designs*

Many people, when they see a beautifully executed piece of quillwork, ask, "How did the artist ever think of that?" and then add, "I could never make anything that looks that good."

But, as we have seen, the techniques for creating even a very complex piece of quilling are really very simple. Margaret Carlson has said that the only real necessity is to have the desire to create. Admittedly, the more elaborate and intricate the creation is, the more time is involved in finishing the project. However, this is true of any art or craft that is well done. The rewards for the time spent at creative work is the joy found in the process of creating, the feeling of accomplishment when the work is complete, and the pleasure in having a lovely finished piece that adds beauty to our lives.

There are many places to find ideas and inspiration for design, among them metal findings catalogs, lace and crochet patterns, jewelry catalogs, cake decorating books, needlepoint designs, and books on ornament design.

Victorian house, Original design by Betty Meisenbach. Artist/Designer, Studio One, St. Louis, Missouri. The artist has given this house unusual treatment by using the quilling strips flat in order to get solidity and vertical lines. Elevation for various extensions of the house is provided by the use of ⅛-inch balsa wood The "gingerbread" of that era is effectively added by the use of standard quilling coils, and the result is another unique style for quillwork.

A second place to start is with a simple outline. This outline can be taken from a child's coloring book, a nature book, a seed catalog, or drawn to your own specification for subject matter. From that point the quiller is free to be fairly precise in filling in the outline, attempting to be accurate in depicting the object; or a bit of whimsy or humor can be added.

Rhinoceros, Joyce Zivic. Joyce drew and filled in this outline of a rhino with a bird on his horn and then added a whimsical touch with white daisies, each with a pastel-colored center, layered on his tough hide.

136

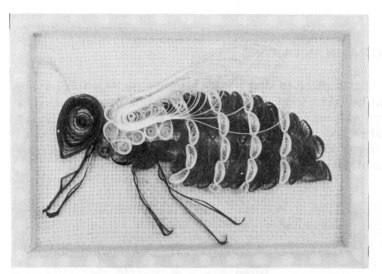

Bee, Frank Tracy. Owned by Laura Davis, Deerfield, Illinois.

Whimsical graceful flower, Grace Wade.

BUILDING A DESIGN ON A FRAME OR COLLAR

One way to begin creating an elaborate design is by building it on a collar. This collar can be of almost any size or shape, and the finished design could frame another small piece of quilling or stand alone. This particular type of quillwork is especially enhanced by a velvet background. The design is built out from the collar in a geometric pattern.

Fran Ann Hamill of Tucson, Arizona, calls the type of collar she uses a skeleton. She makes the skeleton of paper that is cut wider than the strips in the coils. When she has finished her design, she turns the whole piece over. The extra width of the skeleton adds dimension to her finished quilled piece when it is mounted on the background and framed.

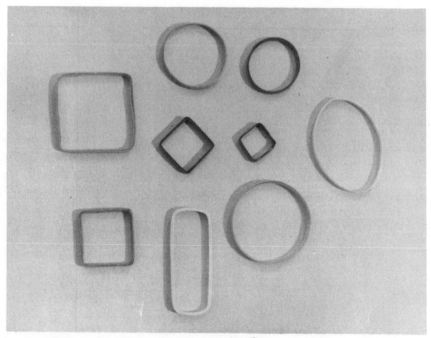

Collars for building up your designs can be made in many sizes and shapes.

Quilled design using collar, Bess R. Baierbach, Cotter, Arkansas. A detail of a design raised from the background by means of a diamond-oval collar on which the design is built. The collar is of wider paper than the quilling strips. Courtesy, Susan B. Alley.

Wedding card, Ruth Richmond, Hinsdale, Illinois. Photograph, Bob Anderson.

A simple, effective "frame within a frame" can be made for photographs. These can be done in a similar manner to building on a collar. However, in order to enhance the photograph rather than overwhelm it, the quillwork around these pictures should be kept simple.

Wedding invitations, birth announcements, meaningful quotations, greeting cards, and other keepsakes can be preserved in a special way by mounting them and decorating them with quillwork. Or, a personal touch can be added to the greeting card itself.

Frame within a frame, Faye Akright, Lee's Summit, Missouri. Seed pearls dress up simple lacy hearts and scrolls to frame this photo. The frame is edged with dark green velvet to match the mat behind the picture. Courtesy, Mrs. A. M. Rumlow, Palatine, Illinois.

Fran Ann Hamill, Tucson, Arizona. Fran Ann calls her finished piece a "Quill."

Jeweled tree, Cleora Carmen. This lacy white tree of hearts and coils is lit by the sparkle of tiny crystal stones.

Sometimes you may find yourself with odd pieces on hand, left over from another project. These can be put together into what is colloquially known as a "just because." "Just because the pieces were there, I glued them together." Other times you may have a frame and a free-form design builds itself to a pleasant piece of quilling that just fits the frame. Or, perhaps you will form a paper outline to be filled with pieces that "just seem to fit." All that remains is to find a background that matches the unusual nature of the quillwork.

Quilling resembling pen an ink drawing, Bernice T. Umland, Albuquerque, New Mexico.

Ladybugs, Judy Farrell. Free-hanging ornaments in natural paper adapt well to all forms of whimsy. Photograph, Bob Anderson.

Nativity in miniature, Barbara Rakovec, B & B Crafts, Windsor, New York. Photograph, Bob Anderson.

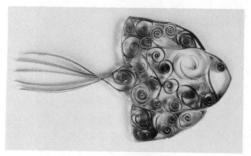

Fish, Virginia Inge, Arlington, Virginia. This whimsical fellow is part of a whole mobile of different sized, multicolored fish.

Candle, Edith J. Schmeisser, Elmhurst, Illinois.

"North Star," ornament, Gene Florida. One of the first innovative 3-D pieces of quilling came from Gene Florida, who began with a square center post of wood from which the quilled design stands out on all four sides. These are accented by tiny pearls and are suspended by a thread from the top of the post. Courtesy, Artistry in Wood, Columbia, Illinois.

Doll in a frame, Juanita Rains, Wichita, Kansas. The doll has quilled flowers in her hand and on her hat. The flowers match the ones in the four corners of the frame.

Aquarium with cork, Lura and Guy Silvernail.

Quilling and tatting, Lora M. Porter, Wichita, Kansas. The lacy gold-colored antique metal frame is a perfect display case for the quilled candles and leaves with the tiny tatted flowers.

Free-form design, Alice Vogel, Albuquerque, New Mexico.

Easter cross with dry pressed flowers,
Grace Wade, Mt. Joy, Pennsylvania.

Maltese cross on a wedgewood plate,
Nell Sterling.

Treasure chest, D. Tracy. An old toy pirate chest bank has been painted white and trimmed with gold braid, quilled flowers, butterflies, and love birds. It was used for a money gift to newlyweds.

Fan, Faye Akright, Lee's Summit, Missouri. Tiny seed pearls are used all over this fan to enhance the quillwork displayed on it.

Oriental screen with quilled border, B. Christy.

Butterfly on a music box, Frank Tracy. Courtesy, Tree Toys, Hinsdale, Illinois. Photograph, Bob Anderson.

*Fuji mums on a gold silk background,
quilling design by Betty Meisenbach
from* Concepts in Quilling, *published
by Cunningham Art Products.*

*Owl, Frank Tracy. This fat owl starts
with a 23-inch strip to make the loose
coil for his body. Eyes and wings are of
11½-inch strips; the head, beak and
cheeks of 5¾-inch strips, and the feet
of 2½-inch strips. Many combinations
of colors can be used.*

150

Cut milk-glass bowl with strawberries, quilling design by Betty Meisenbach from Concepts in Quilling, published by Cunningham Art Products. This quillwork design has a very old-fashioned flavor; the strawberries are done in modern red, vermillion, and hot pink.

Corn, Nell Sterling, Wichita, Kansas. Complete with a hungry mouse eating a kernel in the corner.

Purse, Barbara Maddox, Ballwin, Missouri. Quilled flowers in fall colors and dried grasses are mounted on dark brown velvet or velveteen in this shadow-box purse. Courtesy, Quill Art, Ballwin, Missouri.

Zodiac sign, Bernice T. Umland, Albuquerque, New Mexico. Note her signature—a small "b" quilled in the lower right corner.

152

Fan in a frame, Deane Holder, Wichita, Kansas.

Glass-topped table with fan, Juanita Rains.

Packet steamer, quilling design by
Betty Meisenbach from Concepts In
Quilling, *published by Cunningham
Art Products. This stylized version of
the nostalgic riverboat days uses flat
quilling strips and scrollwork for its
Gothic flavor.*

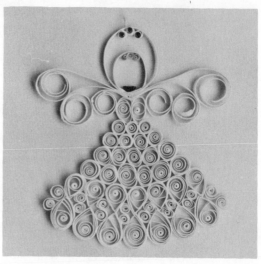

Angel, Louise Denison, Albany, New
York.

Pedestal table, B. Christy. The quill-work is done in white and dark green paper and the edges are gilded. A round glass cut large enough to rest on the table edge protects the paper coils. Photograph, Bob Anderson.

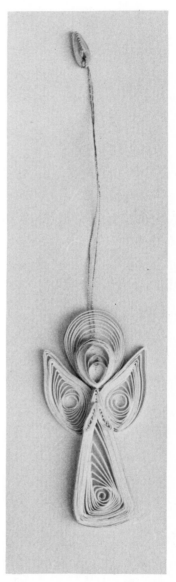

Madonna, Fran Greiner, Mt. Joy, Penn-sylvania.

Mirror, Frank Tracy. Green paper on a gold velvet background. Photograph, Bob Anderson.

Mirror, Frank Tracy. Blue paper with silvered edges, mounted on black velvet. Photograph, Bob Anderson.

Hurricane lamp with quilled grapes, B. Christy and D. Tracy. Photograph, Rayline, Inc., Broadview, Illinois.

Quilled ribbon grapes, ornament, Fran Greiner. The sheen of the satin self-stick ribbon matches the satin ball. The ribbon is split lengthwise and fastened in long strips to make the small coiled pieces. This ornament can be made in lavenders, purples, and reds or in gold, beige, and orange for an effective display of color. Photograph, Bob Anderson.

Quilled ornaments on tree in miniature room, Laura Davis, The Beehive, Deerfield, Illinois.

Pink valentine covered with white quilling touched with gold, Jane Walsh.

Egg with quilled grapes, Jane Walsh, Pownal Center, Vermont.

*Porcelain doll with bread dough flow-
ers, Cora Dyck.*

Porcelain doll (front), Juanita Rains.

Design on velvet, Alice Yahn.

Night light, Juanita Rains.

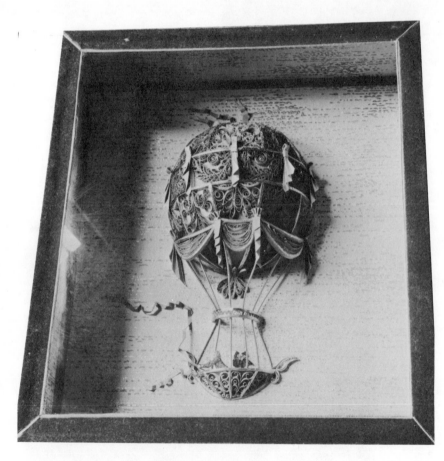

Balloon ascension, Margaret Carlson.

Great horned owl, Frank Tracy.

Cardinal, Frank Tracy.

GEOMETRIC DESIGNS

One place to start creating is with geometric design. This is where the round grid we talked about in Chapter 2 comes in handy. Starting in the center with a round, loose coil, you can build hundreds of variations of the six-pointed snowflake. Start with six of any type of piece you may prefer, and circle the center. The center must be large enough or the pieces small enough to glue them evenly, both to the center piece and to each other. Sometimes it helps to make the six pieces, place them in position, and then make a center to fit them. After the first row is complete, the pieces for the next row can be placed between the pieces of the first row or used as an extension of the first pieces. As the design spreads out from the center, you may want to add connecting pieces in the spaces. A snowflake design can grow to whatever size you want, or it can stop with the first six or seven pieces.

If you start with peacock eyes or diamonds in the center of a geometric form and glue the shapes tip-to-tip, you can begin a four-sided form. Here again, there is room for development, limited only by time available for experimentation and discovery.

In a geometric form, because the combinations of pieces are repeated, the design will almost always be attractive, no matter what assortment of pieces you use. Designs formed from pairs of pieces retain symmetry yet have an unusual, free-form look about them. Much of the fun of designing with quilling is looking for new ways to mix the standard forms and to create something original.

Geometric forms seem to lend themselves especially well to jewelry. Since the pieces are glued everywhere they touch, they give a greater stability to each other and the design. The coils themselves are firm and, with just a little care in handling, quilled jewelry will hold up well.

Bracelet pendant, Elsie Grammer, Chicago, Illinois.

"Just Because."

Geometric design B, Frank Tracy.

Jewelry, Margaret Carlson, Kansas City, Missouri. These elegant pieces of jewelry are made from rolled paper, rolled foil paper, cardboard frames, metal findings, and miscellaneous stones and beads.

Quilled rings with jeweled center, Elsie Grammer, Chicago, Illinois.

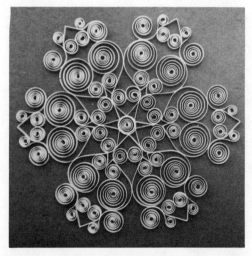

Geometric design A, Frank Tracy. This flake design begins with a loose coil surrounded by six open hearts. The next row is made of twelve variations of the heart glued together to make six pairs. The outer row consists of clusters of two "S" variations and an open heart. Note that the open coils have a very airy effect.

167

7 Patterns for Quilling

In this chapter, we will present several patterns for you to follow. We hope our patterns will inspire you to create your own designs.

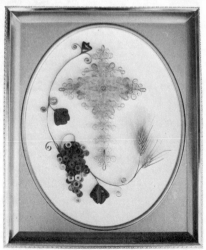

Symbols of religious faith, Fran Greiner, Mt. Joy, Pennsylvania. The cross, grapes, and wheat are the symbols that have been combined in a delicate reverent picture.

168

The cross is of white paper. After it is complete, spray with
clear acrylic to seal. Mount cross on art-paper background
and spray very lightly with gold so that some of the gold spray
adds a shadow to the background.

This design is built on a wider strip formed into a round collar. Each of the paper strips for the coils is about the same length. Contrast is provided by the use of round closed coils and peacock eyes for closed areas and "S" shapes for the open areas. When the design is complete, turn the whole piece over for mounting. The collar will hold the design away from the background.

The long grasses are made by folding a 23-inch strip
in half and gluing the two sides flat together. Glue eleven or
twelve of the double strips flat together at one end and cut to
various lengths. The double strips are heavy enough to be
shaped gently as though a bunch of grasses were gathered
together. The cattails are circles of about 1½ inch strips
formed into ovals. Their stems are made like the grasses with
one end left open and glued to the cattail. The blossoms are
diamond and leaf shapes made from 23-inch and 11½ inch
strips of black. The bowl is made of squares of 23-inch strips
of black in the front and 11½ inch strips in the back, with
spaces for the flower and grass stems to fit in. The base is a 23-
inch strip of black bent into a tulip shape.

*Pileated woodpeckers,
Anna Harding,
Elmhurst, Illinois.*

In this design the tree trunk and branches are gray and the leaves are green. The three coils on the head of each bird marked with an X are to be made of red paper. The coils that have a line in the center are black. The others are white.

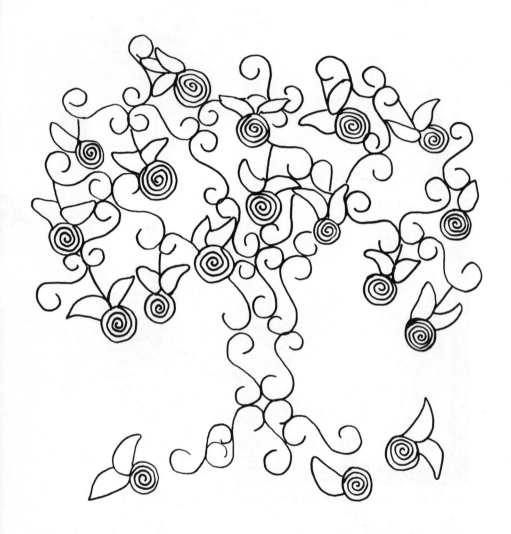

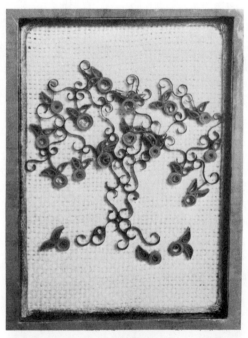

Apple tree, Anita K. Bate, Glenview, Illinois. This little apple tree is patterned after a needlepoint design. The "S" shapes in the trunk and branches are black, the leaves are green, and the apples are red.

Pintail duck, Lura and Guy Silvernail, Syracuse, New York. Much of the shading in the feathers of this duck is done by rolling colors together or starting a coil with one color and finishing with another. Quite subtle shading can be done in this manner.

MIRROR

Frank Tracy of Hinsdale, Illinois, has provided us with a step-by-step procedure for making a framed mirror.

The frame selected for this piece is a 14- by 11-inch oval frame (the measurements refer to the glass, which fits into the frame from the back). The glass is standard $\frac{3}{32}$-inch picture frame glass, cut to fit at a frame store. The mirror glass is $\frac{1}{8}$ inch thick.

Other materials include basswood ($\frac{1}{8}$ inch thick) and a luxurious piece of velvet or velveteen of a suitable color. For this mirror, the material used was burgundy velvet. An oval piece measuring slightly less than 11 by 14 inches is the size needed.

For assembling the mirror you will also need a clear-drying white glue, an epoxy glue, construction paper, graph paper, wax paper, corrugated cardboard, $\frac{3}{8}$-inch #4 flat head wood screws, glazier's points, a ruler, yardstick, pins, scissors, quilling tool, and paper.

1. To make an 11 by 14 inch oval pattern of construction paper, place the frame face up on the construction paper and outline the *inner* oval, which rests on the paper. Cut along the line. The oval paper should fit smoothly and exactly, into the space later to be occupied by the glass. This pattern is used to cut ovals of the correct size of wax paper, corrugated cardboard, $\frac{1}{8}$ inch basswood, graph paper, and velvet. All of these ovals should fit as accurately as possible into the frame.

2. Using the pattern, cut out an oval of basswood. It will be about the size of the glass and is used as backing for the velvet. Cut a larger oval of $\frac{1}{8}$-inch basswood the same size as the back of the frame, using the frame itself as the pattern. Sand and seal both pieces of wood.

3. Carefully and accurately fold the construction paper pattern in half. Draw a line along the crease. Then fold in half the opposite way and draw along the crease. The pattern will thus be marked off in equal quarters.

Mirror, Frank Tracy, Hinsdale, Illinois.

180

Making an oval pattern.

Pattern, frame, and backings.

Marking the frame.

181

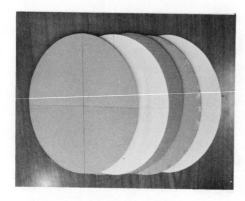

Pattern and ovals.

Centering the mirror.

Outside border.

182

4. Place the pattern in the frame and, using the guidelines, mark the back of the frame at its top, bottom and sides. Draw a light pencil line on the inner edge at these points to serve as a guide to placing quilled pieces.

5. Cut out an oval of graph paper, with ¼-inch divisions, using the pattern. Take care to see that one of the vertical lines on the graph paper corresponds to the longest diameter line of the oval pattern and accentuate this line with a pencil. Similarly, match and mark in the shortest diameter. The graph paper will then be marked into equal quarters with exact top, bottom, and sides located.

6. Using the pattern, cut out two ovals of corrugated cardboard and an oval of wax paper. Place the oval of graph paper on one of the cardboard ovals with the wax paper oval on top. Fasten them with transparent tape and insert them into the frame from the back with the wax paper toward the front. If all has gone well, the diameter lines accentuated on the graph paper will coincide with the lightly drawn pencil lines on the inner edge of the frame. Put the other oval of cardboard in back of these pieces to hold them in place and tape it to the frame with masking tape.

7. Place the mirror face down on the wax paper and center it with a ruler. With a felt pen, draw the outline of the mirror on the wax paper to aid in relocating it if it slips. Pins stuck into the cardboard around the mirror will help hold it in place.

8. Now you are ready to quill pieces and arrange them in whatever borders and patterns are pleasing to you.

The design pictured contains about 240 quilled pieces. The scroll-like pieces used are described in Chapter 3. The larger pieces were made from strips of paper about 5¾ inches long. The smaller ones are from strips about 2⅞ inches long. The quotes in the chalice and butterfly, the large hearts, the petals, and leaves of the daisy, and the outer petals of the rose are all made from strips about 5¾ inches long. The tulips and the center of the rose were made from strips 11½ inches long, and the lily flowers were molded from a loose coil made from 1½-inch strips. Hollow circles were formed around a ⅜-inch dowel, starting with a 1-inch strip.

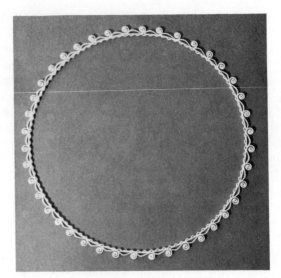

Inside border.

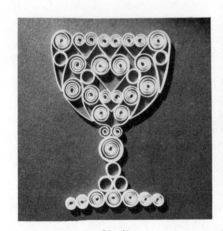

Chalice.

Butterfly.

When making quilled pieces for a border and symmetrical items like the chalice or butterfly, practice until you can turn out the desired number of pieces close to the same size and shape. Though irregular pieces can be assembled in a variety of pleasing ways, for this purpose some degree of similarity looks better. The graph paper helps balance the pattern as the pieces are made and fitted in.

Glue together only sections that can be lifted out and returned to their proper position later when the quilling is glued to the velvet.

Finish the design and arrange it as it will appear in the final stage. Move pieces about until the desired effect is achieved and pin the glued sections in place.

9. Using the original construction paper pattern, cut out an oval of velvet or other material. Press out the wrinkles. Spray with Scotchguard and allow to dry.

10. Glue the velvet to the smaller oval of basswood. If you use epoxy glue in the center area, which will be covered by the mirror, you will insure that the mirror won't slip. The outer area of velvet can be glued with the same clear white glue used for quilling. Spread the glue evenly but lightly.

11. Remove the cardboard with the quilled pattern from the frame. Remove the mirror and clean it. Leave the quilled pieces pinned to the front cardboard oval. Remove the other cardboard oval. Place the velvet-covered wood into the frame. Mark the back of the wood and the frame so that, when it is replaced, it can be lined up with these marks and returned to the exact same position. Place one of the cardboard ovals behind the wood to hold it in place, and secure with masking tape.

12. Place the mirror in the center of the velvet and locate it evenly with a ruler. Push a few pins through the velvet into the wood at the edge of the mirror. These pins will guide the mirror back to its center placement after the glue is applied. Glue with epoxy glue.

13. Transfer the quilled pieces to the velvet and, when they are arranged where you want them, glue the sections together and glue the sections to the velvet. Use white glue that dries clear. Be neat. Don't mess up the velvet.

*Gluing the velvet
with epoxy glue.*

*Gluing the outer
edge of velvet.*

Completed design.

14. Remove the cardboard and the wooden oval with its quilling, velvet, and mirror face. Clean and insert the glass, fastening it adequately with glazier's points.

15. Remove fuzz, lint, etc., from the velvet. Re-insert the art work, lining up the marks on the back of the wood with those on the frame. If you have been careful, the quilled pieces will be in their same relative positions to the frame as when you glued them to the velvet.

16. Place the back (the larger basswood oval) over the art work backing and secure to the frame with the small screws through predrilled holes. If the back does not lay flush on the back of the frame because the glass and art work inserts are too thick, use one or two small washers around each screw between the back and the frame. This relieves the pressure on the glass.

The quilling tends to "slide" on the nap of the velvet. Thus, when the quilling is pushed against the glass from behind, it may drift. This is kept to a minimum by firm but not messy gluing of the border. This is also the reason for the washers.

17. The edge of the wood backing can be covered with a strip of braid to match the frame. The braid is glued around the edge of the backing when the mirror is completely assembled.

Daisy and rose.

Tulips and lily-of-the-valley.

EGG

Perhaps the first quilled egg was made by Mary Keyes of McLean, Virginia. The egg is 5 inches tall and measures 9 inches around. Made of a fine paper, off-white in color, it looks like carved ivory and stands on a tall gold egg stand. It needs to be kept under a glass dome to protect it from dust and handling, as it is quite fragile. The completed egg contains from 350 to 400 quilled pieces made on a corsage pin. The diamond shapes make daisy designs, which are joined together with open hearts, loose coils, and "S" shapes. The pieces are of 1-, 2-, or 3-inch strips to keep them small. Mary designed the egg while she was in the process of making it.

For those who are inclined to try a project like this, Mary Keyes has outlined the steps.

1. Mark the goose egg in half (upright) and work only one side at a time.

2. Keep the center line irregular so there will not be a noticeable straight line when the two sides are put together.

3. Try to match both sides in design.

4. Attach some of the quilled pieces to the shell with a tiny dot of glue to aid in following the egg shape. The shapes are easily pried off of the shell with the corsage pin when half the egg is quilled.

5. Quill the two sides and remove. Put the two sides together with open hearts, loose coils and "S" shapes.

The egg took about fifteen hours of working time to complete.

Lacy whole quilled egg, Mary Keyes, McLean, Virginia.

189

Ornamental egg, Margaret Carlson, Kansas City, Missouri. The egg shape is formed of cardboard dividers covered with gold embossed papers and filled with quilled pieces. Around the center are tiny, old-fashioned pictures.

Quilled egg with stained-glass window, Ruth Richmond. Photograph, Bob Anderson.

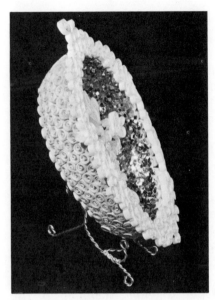

Quilled egg: side view, Ruth Richmond. Photograph, Bob Anderson.

Panoramic, brightly colored egg on plastic form, Arlene Spriggs Trujillo. Courtesy, International Leisure Activities, Inc., Springfield, Ohio. Photograph, Arthur C. Frock.

191

CATHEDRAL

Another first in quilling is this church made by Ruth Richmond of Hinsdale, Illinois. The number of pieces is unknown, but the church stands about 15½ inches high to the top of the cross. It is 5 inches wide and 6½ inches from front to back. Other heights are 14 inches to the top of the steeple, 7¼ inches to the peak of the roof. The fence posts are 1⅞ inches high. The church stands on a 14½ by 10½-inch piece of styrofoam covered with artificial grass. The tiny fence is supported by toothpicks. It took about six weeks of evenings to build. The church also needs to be kept under glass for protection. The idea was inspired by a cake decorating design. The windows of this cathedral are covered with a stained glass window paper; and inside are some tiny pews and an altar.

To make this cathedral, it would be well to prepare a cardboard pattern that can be taped together, standing up. The cardboard sections can then be traced, in outline, onto paper patterns, and the church can be made section by section.

The back and sides of this church are made of small round coils, bordered with tight coils and glued in rows to form the wall, with openings left for windows (also outlined with tight coils).

The front of the church and openings are outlined in tight coils and the design is made of a number of other coils with the spaces filled in with peacock eyes, scrolls, and "S" shapes.

The roof is made of two large sections, outlined and crisscrossed by rows of round coils. The areas in between are fitted with peacock eyes that all point toward the center.

When all the sections are built, they can be carefully butted up against each other and glued securely in place. The church will be stronger if every coil that touches another coil is fastened to it with a small drop of glue.

Cathedral, Ruth Richmond, Hinsdale,
Illinois. Photograph, Bob Anderson.

Front view of old caddy showing miss-
ing coils and convex glass dome over a
painting on silk. The original lock and
key are intact. The tea caddy dates
about 1790.

Back and side views of old tea caddy.

Rolled paper picture, English. Queen Anne. Dated 1710. 17⅞ by 16½ inches. This heraldic crest is made of red paper with gilt edges mounted on a rust velvet backing. Courtesy, Art Institute of Chicago.

195

Suppliers

Artistry in Wood
  (Wholesale Only)
Gene Florida
P.O. Box 131
Columbia, Illinois 62236
	Kits
	Paper
	Instruction "Filigree
	  Paper Art"

Beach Co., Ltd.
  (Wholesale Only)
P.O. Box 190
Fort Meyers, Florida 33902
	Quillo Paper
	Instruction "Quilling
	  by Dorothy"

Marilyn Bell 4021 N. Cherry Kansas City, Missouri 64116	Booklet "An Ancient Art Quilling"
J. L. Brown Company (Wholesale Only) P.O. Box 27341 Creve Coeur, Missouri 63141	Paper Patterns
Carols Crafts, Inc. (Wholesale Only) Carol and Pete Dreesen 8652 Magnolia Avenue Santee, California 92071	Paper Quillcraft Kits Instruction Pads Books
Craft Course Publishers, Inc. Rosemead, California	Book "Decorative Quilling" Book "The Art of Quilling"
Creative Corner, Inc. (Wholesale Only) 3701 No. Ravenswood Ave. Chicago, Illinois 60613	Kits

Cunningham Art Products, Inc.
  (Wholesale Only)
1555 Roadhaven Drive   Kits
Stone Mountain, Georgia 30083 Book "Concepts in Quilling"

Fireside Shopper
Mary M. Ilewski
Rt. 2   Kits
Gerald, Missouri 63037   Paper

Fran Ann Hamill
642 Roller Coaster Road
Tucson, Arizona 85704   Book "My Kind of Quill"

R. B. Howell Company
  (Wholesale Only)   Quillcraft Instructions
630 Northwest 10th Ave.   Patterns
Portland, Oregon 97209   Paper

International Leisure Activities Inc.
  (Wholesale Only)
Arlene Spriggs Trujillo   Dimensional Kits
309 North Plum Street   Paper
Springfield, Ohio 45504   Pattern Sheets

J. D. J. Designs
Lori Muhrline
Lori's Arts and Crafts
1154 Manchester Road   Kits

Manchester, Missouri 63011   Paper

Leone Originals
  (Wholesale Only)
P.O. Box 275
Bensenville, Illinois 60106   Paper

Linda's Quilling
Linda Ebersole
521 Luella
Mulvane, Kansas 67110   Paper

Harold Mangelsen & Sons, Inc.
  (Wholesale Only)   Paper
8200 "J" Street   Book "Quilling"
Omaha, Nebraska 68127   Quilling Tools

Hazel Pearson Handicrafts   Paper, Work Board
  (Wholesale Only)   Quill Quicky, Curling Tools
4128 Temple City Boulevard   Books "Decorative Quilling"
Rosemead, California 91770   "New Designs for Quilling"

Priceless Pastimes Art Co., Ltd.   Paper, Precious Jewels
Virginia G. Antoine   "Priceless Pastimes Heir-
12101 Newbury Lane   loom Treasures Quilling
Independence, Missouri 64052   Books" Vol. I and II

Quaint Quilling
Dixie Miller and Rose Ann Sloan
P.O. Box 17204
Orlando, Florida 32810   Book "Quaint Quilling"

Quill Art   Paper, Kits
  (Wholesale Only)   Quilling Glue
Barbara Maddox   Books "It's Your Turn to
852 Gardenway Drive   Quill" — "It's Your Turn
Ballwin, Missouri 63011   to Quill Some More"

Quilling Bee Enterprises   Paper
Betty Nelson   Patterns
4004 Fairway Court   Book "The Four Seasons
Arlington, Texas 76013   of Quilling"

Rapco, Inc.
   (Wholesale Only)
500 No. Spaulding Ave.
Chicago, Illinois 60624   Kits

Gunter Stave
Leisure Services
P.O. Box 2763   Book "The Art of Quilling"
Kansas City, Missouri 64142   (1966)

Studio Craft
   (Wholesale Only)
1840 No. Clybourn Avenue
Chicago, Illinois 60614   Kits

Tree Toys   Paper, Kits
P.O. Box 492   Books "Introducing Quilling"
Hinsdale, Illinois 60521   "Christmas Quilling"

Lee Wards   Kits
Elgin, Illinois 60120   Paper

Christopher York, Inc.
   (Wholesale Only)
5875 No. Lincoln Avenue
Chicago, Illinois 60659   Kits

Zims
   (Wholesale Only)
240 East 2nd Street   Paper
Salt Lake City, Utah 84111   Instruction Sheets

Museums that Show Quilling

UNITED STATES

The Art Institute of Chicago
Michigan Avenue at Adams Street
Chicago, Illinois 60603

Beauport House in Gloucester,
Massachusetts
The Society for the Preservation
of New England Antiquities
141 Cambridge Street
Boston, Massachusetts 02114

Colonial Williamsburg Foundation
Williamsburg, Virginia 23185

Essex Institute
132-4 Essex Street
Salem, Massachusetts 01970

The Golden Ball Tavern
Boston Post Road, Box 223
Weston, Massachusetts 02193

Henry Ford Museum
Oakwood Boulevard
Dearborn, Michigan 48121

Henry Francis DuPont Winterthur
Museum
Winterthur, Delaware 19735

Historic Deerfield, Inc.
Sheldon-Hawks Museum House
Deerfield, Massachusetts 01342

Metropolitan Museum of Art
Fifth Avenue and 82nd Street
New York, New York 10028

Museum of Fine Arts
Huntington Avenue
Boston, Massachusetts 02115

The Sappington House Foundation
1015 South Sappington Road
Crestwood, Missouri 63126

Worcester Art Museum
55 Salisbury Street
Worcester, Massachusetts 01608

EUROPE

Le Musee Arlaten
Arles, France

Lady Lever Art Gallery
Port Sunlight
Cheshire, England

Victoria and Albert Museum
South Kensington
London SW7, England

200

Bibliography

Creekmore, Betsey B., *Traditional American Crafts*, Great Neck, New York: Hearthside, 1971.

Eckstein, Artis Aleene, and Shannon, Alice, *How to Make Treasures from Trash*, Great Neck, New York: Hearthside, 1972.

Edwards, Ralph, "Filigree Paper Decoration," in *The Dictionary of English Furniture*, London: Country Life, Ltd., 1954.

Gaines, Edith, "Collector's Notes," *Antiques*, October 1962, 410-411.

Gaines, Edith, "Collector's Notes," *Antiques*, February 1970, 272-274.

Gaines, Edith, "Minor Arts: Quillwork, Treen, Chalkware," in *The Concise Encyclopedia of American Antiques*, New York: Hawthorne, 1957.

Gaines, Edith, "Quillwork: American Paper Filigree," *Antiques*, December 1960, 562-565.

Harrower, Dorothy, *Decoupage—A Limitless World in Decoration*, Bonanza, 1958.

Haslein, Inge, and Frischmann, Rita, *Curling Coiling and Quilling*, New York: Sterling, 1973.

Hughes, G. Bernard, "Rolled Paper Art," *Country Life* 60:2853 (21 September 1951), 894-895.

Johnson, Pauline, *Creating with Paper*, Seattle: University of Washington Press, 1958.

Johnson, R. Brimley, "The Flora of Mrs. Delany," *The Connoisseur*, 78:312, 220-227.

Morse, Frances Clary, *Furniture of the Olden Time*, New York: Macmillan, 1936.

Newman, Jay Hartley, Lee Scott, and Thelma R., *Paper as Art and Craft*, New York: Crown, 1973.

Rothery, Guy Cadogan, "Rolled Paper Work," *Antiques*, July 1929, 21-24.

Acknowledgments

In our search for quillwork, old and new, we have been delighted by the spirit of cooperation and sharing that we encountered with everyone we met, spoke to, or wrote. We are especially indebted to Dona Meilach of Palos Heights, Illinois, who gave us unprecedented assistance out of her own experience in research and authoring. We thank Jackie Watson of Crescent City, Illinois, for being our first respondent and starting us off with hope; Barbara Brabec of *Artisan Crafts* for keeping aware of and finding quillers; Esther Rebman of Lancaster, Pennsylvania, for putting us in touch with many people in that area; and Mrs. A. Roy Brenneman of Lancaster for her instant hospitality.

We are grateful to Bonnie Nagle of Pittsford, New York, for contributing all her notes on quilling design; Bill Christy, Jr., of Denver, Colorado, for the loan of his camera for so many months; Bob Anderson of Hinsdale, Illinois, for his photographic contributions; Don Buckley of Illinois Bronze Products for taking some last minute photographs; and Mike Johnson of Hinsdale, Illinois, for his aid with drawings.

Our appreciation goes to Helen O'Neill, of the Hinsdale Public Library, for finding every reference no matter how elusive; Helen Jean LaForce of Hinsdale, Illinois, for her efforts on our behalf in Europe; A. P. Burton, Assistant Keeper of the Library, Victoria and Albert Museum, London, for his help with references; and M. Guy Selz of Paris, for his additional information.

We remember with pleasure Lora Porter and the Quilling Guild of Wichita, Kansas, for their enthusiasm and support; and Margaret Carlson of Kansas City, Missouri, for her inspiration.

On technical matters, we are indebted to J. R. Dryden of Carnival Crafts, Hinsdale, Illinois, for time and materials for experimentation; and Charles Krubl and Richard Simak of Rayline, Inc., Broadview, Illinois, for helping untangle our photographic problems.

202

We are appreciative of the response we received from quilling suppliers, especially Artistry in Wood; Cunningham Art Products Inc.; International Leisure Activities, Inc.; J.D.J. Designs, Manchester, Missouri; Priceless Pastimes Co., Ltd. Quill Art; Quilling Bee Enterprises; and Quaint Quilling who contributed designs and encouragement.

Everyone who is a part of this book has been responsive; and Louise Denison, Fran Greiner, Virginia Inge, Guy and Lura Silvernail, Phyllis LeMar, and Jane Walsh we appreciate for a little extra.

We thank our families for their moral support and cheering us on, and especially Paul for lending a hand at important times.

Quilling is a new art, and every day more people are discovering it. Because of this rapid growth, we have been unable to include in this book all the excellent quilling that has been done. The authors would be grateful for any information on both old and new quilling that readers can provide. Letters should be sent to Tree Toys (address in supply list).

Index